Rediscoveries: Literature and Place in Illinois

ROBERT C. BRAY

Rediscoveries: Literature and Place in Illinois

UNIVERSITY OF ILLINOIS PRESS

Urbana Chicago London

The following publishers, authors, and holders of copyright have generously
given their permission to quote from copyrighted materials: the editors of
The Old Northwest for "Robert Herrick: A Chicago Trio" (1[Mar. 1975])
and "The Mystical Landscape: Francis Grierson's *The Valley of Shadows*"
(5[Winter 1979-80]); the editors of *The Great Lakes Review* for "Hamlin
Garland's *Rose of Dutcher's Coolly*" (Summer 1976); John Judson and the
Center for Contemporary Poetry for Lisel Mueller's "Highway 2, Illinois"
from *Voyages to the Inland Sea,* vol. 1; James McGowan for "On Writing an
Illinois Poem"; Dave Etter for "Bright Mississippi" from *Bright Mississippi,*
"Michael Flanagan" from *Cornfields,* "Ancestral Home" and "Hotel Tall
Corn" from *Alliance, Illinois,* and "Forgotten Graveyard" from *Heartland:
Poets of the Midwest* (ed. Lucien Stryk); the Family Trust of Carl Sandburg
for "Chicago," "Mill-Doors," "Onion Days," and "Subway" from *Chicago
Poems;* and Harper and Row for William Stafford's "Lake Chelan," "In
Response to a Question," and "Prairie Town" from *Stories That Could Be
True* (1977).

LIBRARY OF CONGRESS CATALOGING IN PUBLICATION DATA

Bray, Robert C.
    Rediscoveries: Literature and place in Illinois.

    Includes index.
    1. American literature—Illinois—History and
criticism. 2. Illinois in literature. I.   title.
PS283.I3B7   810'.9'9773   81-3353
ISBN 0-252-00911-8   AACR2

On Writing An Illinois Poem

I shouldn't do it yet;
   don't know this place,
      I've been here now three years and don't relate.

One notes things, though:
   the squares—of land that is;
      the prairie's laid in blocks
      and towns are just a smaller grid;
      roads meet in perpendicular
      and go in only four directions
         (though a thousand miles in each).

I've heard the flatlands give one scope and room to breathe—
   but how the horizon circles you, a matter of fact:
   huge clouds, torrents, tornadoes lower and zero in;
      it's time to pray, it's time to hide in cellars.
Or summer nights the field dust hides the stars like cities' smog.

Here, on the prairie's best days,
   there is nothing for the mind to climb on;
   it grows tassel high and reachable,
      grows always grounded,
      grows to be brought down in its cycle,
      re-grown in old grooves
   by these minds contained, steel-clad,
      stores of the dry wisdom of fact and practice,
         who dominate the innocent attention
         as grain elevators command the highway.
(And there are men whose fields grow tall,
      while houses crack in years of wind
      and children split and wrinkle, die in their rows.)

In trying writing
   I can sense the spirit of the place
   resists the secretive, the singular, mysterious—the thoughtful—
but I think of men who first stepped from the shelter of the woods
   onto the prairie—

did they ever lose that prickling in their necks,
    that metaphysical prickle?
    such a private thing, but thus
    they did, I think unquestioned duty
    in the center of that bullseye,
and still their qualities—submission, routine, struggle—
    are those most pertinent to men who walk these squares and rows
        under the circling sky.

But yet I understand so few things of this land and people—
    flats and facts and squares—
        I should not write.
I think, though, that there is
    there must be mystery, dimension, depth—
        each citizen his soul, each grid its ghosts—
I've heard of towering substance, strength, imagination,
prairie art, and love—
    (and rumors of the circles and the symbols out of sight,
    behind thick blinds,
    in dark, in woody parlors).

                                  —James McGowan

Acknowledgments

These "essays in rediscovery" began with a commission several years ago from the Center for Illinois Studies. As early as 1974, Bruce Thomas, the center's founder and director, had envisioned a series of monographs on Illinois history and culture which, he hoped, would collectively make an important contribution to Illinois's celebration of the American Bicentennial. Of idealism and energy Bruce and the center had plenty; of money, unfortunately, there was considerably less. Hence most of the manuscripts associated with this laudable enterprise never reached print. Nonetheless, I want to thank Bruce Thomas for getting me started—and for continuing his encouragement to this day.

Along the way to publication several earlier versions of chapters have appeared in scholarly journals. In particular I wish to thank the editors of *The Great Lakes Review* and *The Old Northwest* for their kind permission to adapt and reprint this material. Likewise, thanks are due to John Judson, of the Center for Contemporary Poetry at the University of Wisconsin, La Crosse, for permission to quote both poetry and prose from his invaluable series, *Voyages to the Inland Sea*. And, of course, thanks to the Carl Sandburg estate for permission to quote from *Chicago Poems*.

I am especially obliged to my faculty colleagues here at Illinois Wesleyan, who deemed this project worthy of support through a Faculty Research Grant, and to the University administration for a generous contribution toward publication costs.

To my good friend and sometime coauthor, Paul Bushnell, heartfelt thanks: he read and criticized the manuscript and kept me going during the doubtful times. And thanks as well to Alberta Carr, for her expert preparation of the manuscript for submission to the publisher.

Finally, special thanks to James McGowan and Dave Etter—a poet in

Illinois and an Illinois poet—for their generosity in allowing me to use entire poems at the beginning and at the end of *Literature and Place in Illinois*. "On Writing an Illinois Poem" is the epigraph, "Roots" the envoy—and the book profits a great deal from their epitomizing power.

Contents

Literary Archaeology

> If there were no names in the history of art except those belonging to the creators of new forms there would be no culture. The very word implies a continuity, and therefore it calls for disciples, imitators and followers to make a living chain; in other words, a tradition.
>
> —André Gide

The Literary Prospect

In the first expansive years following the conclusion of America's second war with Great Britain, new settlers streamed into the largely vacant Illinois country. The tributaries of this great migrant flow were New England, Ohio, the South. And on every tongue, in every expectant heart, was the talismanic word "Land!" To the nineteenth-century American the land which beckoned him westward symbolized a stout yeoman's freedom in an incipient agricultural empire. For uncounted people land, and land alone, was the key to a competency. We can no longer wholly comprehend the manner in which land was emotionally compelling and formative of cultural expectations, and this is true no matter how earnestly we romanticize the idea and the fact of emigration. Imagine one of those families moving slowly across the face of the land from Pennsylvania: the Ephraim Prouders—father, wife and mother named Selina, adolescent son quixotically named Usury, and a sickly, anonymous little girl not likely to survive the winter. They had loaded up their possessions and undertaken that westward journey which has become as central to the American mythos as the Exodus to the Hebrews. The family's goal was Spring County, Illinois—there, as they thought, to claim "six hundred 'n' forty acres o' the finest land th't ever laid ou' doors." Part of this garden plot the elder Prouder had earned from hav-

1

ing "fit" the British in the late war; the rest he would get "fee simple," and the hopes of the family could scarcely have been higher as they made mile after tedious mile across Indiana toward their homestead. Of course, they hardly foresaw the excruciating toil and the catalogue of human miseries that lay ahead, for they, as so many others, were acting from a belief system which naively held that successful farming might be done by any American hearty enough and with a will, just so long as the land was to be had. And in their case the land was undeniably there, a shock to them—it was treeless, something called "prairie"—but nonetheless glorious to their eyes, and all but illimitable.

While the Prouders were among the early inhabitants of "Spring County, Illinois," they never existed as persons. They and their county were, and are, fictional entities in the universe of a little-known nineteenth-century novel called *Zury: The Meanest Man in Spring County.* *Zury* was written by an Illinois lawyer and dabbler in numerous trades, including authorship, to which he devoted only the later years of his life and of which this novel was the first and best fruit. Joseph Kirkland is today unknown to all but the most inveterate novel-readers, but his novel of frontier Illinois life was brought out in 1887 by a reputable New York publishing house and, though hardly a sensation, may be said to have gained a national audience for Illinois-based literature. But the striking thing to a modern reader of Kirkland's novel is that it was written not at all contemporaneously with the events it described. From the heights of postbellum midwestern civilization, from the very center of the Gilded Age, the Age of Excess, the Chromo civilization, the novel looks retrospectively at the early years of settlement some three-quarters of a century previous. Those intervening years had witnessed in Illinois the same untrammeled growth that had been characteristic of the entire heart of the nation: first the establishment of the agrarian West, the "fee-simple empire" and the "Garden of the World" as it has been termed, then the disruption of the Civil War, and afterward the astonishing surge of industrialization and concomitant urbanization which inevitably meant the cultural decline of the yeoman farmer and his milieu. By the time Joseph Kirkland came to try his hand at making art out of the homely materials of rural Illinois, the focus of state and national culture had long since shifted to Chicago and other cities and seemed unlikely ever to return to the countryside again. Kirkland himself had given up his downstate existence in favor of Chicago's challenge, and he was aware that composition for him involved acts of memory not only over time but over space as well.

Here, then, is a fundamental fact about the rural literature of rural Illinois: it is postbellum, postagrarian and, most importantly, filtered through the roseate atmosphere of retrospection. Books like *Zury* have a quite specific range of tone and subject matter. They would make the homely heroic and attempt to paint their frontier people in a palette of melancholy and bucolic tones which derive from the realization that a seminal way of life is no more and a belief that this loss is too bad. These books are the romances of prairie and grove and river bottom, written not, to be sure, in the mode of James Fenimore Cooper's *Leather-Stocking Tales,* where History is always uppercase, nor in the manner of the popular sentimental romance, where Virtue is always and in every way rewarded. Rather the romance in such pieces is the native American ritual drama of the creation from prairie and woods of the yeoman's quarter-section homestead and farm: the clearing of the land, the communal house-raising, the sowing of winter wheat, the first harsh winter in Illinois with its attendant climatic sicknesses, then the spring with the first crop breaking through the prairie soil, and finally the long-anticipated initial harvest. Was the gathering meager or bountiful? *That* incalculable question supplied the romance that made the agrarian novel such an enduring part of our fiction, finding perhaps its noblest expression in Rolvaag's *Giants in the Earth,* but in any case finally transcending regionalism and following the frontier westward, all the way to California—the San Joaquin Valley becomes the setting for Frank Norris's *The Octopus* (1903), the first volume in his "Epic of the Wheat."

But how, given this aura of romance informing the agrarian novel in Illinois and elsewhere, can we account for the minute attention to realistic, workaday detail that is also characteristic of the work of writers such as Joseph Kirkland? Any explanation of the relationship between realism and romanticism must be complex rather than simple, for the writers with whom these essays will be concerned worked in a welter of socioartistic forces that belies the monolithic picture not infrequently given of American literature between the Civil War and World War I: the so-called Age of Realism. It is certainly true that the realistic aesthetic was in the ascendant for a number of decades after the Civil War, and not only in America but in Europe. The United States produced two great prophets of literary realism, Henry James and William Dean Howells. They were able to reach a national audience both through their novels and in the critical writing which appeared in the pages of such influential magazines as the *Atlantic, Harper's,* and the *Century.* It was particularly William Dean Howells who became associated with the school of native

American realism, became in fact its mentor and paternal symbol—the man and the artist to whom, by 1880, young writers from all over the country were looking for solace, support, and a kind review from his "editor's easy chair." Howells was in the enviable position of having the nation's ear when it came to literary pronouncements, and he was fond of defining American realism in literature as "nothing more and nothing less than the truthful treatment of material." No matter that this popular dictum collapsed an entire set of tough philosophical questions about literary form, content, and technique: it was nevertheless the guiding principle for two generations of American novelists, and it retained a dogmatic force in our letters at least until World War I and perhaps beyond.

"Nothing more and nothing less than the truthful treatment of material" ... "The illusion of reality in art" ... "Let only the truth be told." Such doctrines surely molded the writers of the heartland as much as they preoccupied the literati of Boston and New York. For in this vast and amorphous region called the Midwest—actually the Old Northwest and the Great Plains combined—there were not lacking after the Civil War young and ambitious artists whose optimistic goal was the articulation of their land. In the famous phrase of Hamlin Garland, what they sought was a "distinctive utterance" for the Midwest. Not all, or even necessarily the best, of these hopefuls hailed from Illinois, nor were they all especially interested in agrarian fiction. Their unity consisted in a devotion to a vision of cultural identity which, as it did not already exist, demanded to be created from the materials at hand. Each state in the Midwest had its representative authors. On the Great Plains a pair of newspaper-editors-turned-novelists were helping put Kansas into the national consciousness. William Allen White of Emporia, while much better known as a stalwart of the Republican party, devoutly wished to be remembered as a progressive in his fiction, which was evocative of the horse and buggy era after the Civil War, the "simpler" time before the onset of industrialism and before the folk wisdom of small Kansas towns began to be viewed as merely quaint. And up in Atchison Edgar Watson Howe, the misanthropic "Sage of Potato Hill," as he was known to the locals, wrote more darkly—sometimes even gothically—of the other side of the Kansas equation: loneliness, cultural deprivation, and personal arrested development. The state of Nebraska had the young Willa Cather (though it was only many years later, after she made her national reputation, that they would boast of the fact), whose career was in effect beginning about the time the Kansas editors were drying up artistically. Iowa might claim as a native son Hamlin Garland, but had to share him with Wisconsin and Illinois—in fact, with the entire Middle Border from the "Coolly country" to the long corn rows to the city of Chicago. As one moved eastward from the plains into the Mississippi and Ohio Valleys, the culture naturally got older and more settled. Here the profession of letters was the eldest: Edward Eggleston had published his first novel of the region, the celebrated *Hoosier Schoolmaster*, in 1871, and had managed to increase his fame with each succeeding book of local color fiction, a series of seven culminating in *The Graysons* (subtitled *A Story of Abraham Lincoln*) in 1887. And by the 1890s there was already a second generation of Ohio Valley writers, building upon the work of the first and, so they earnestly thought, materially improving upon it as well. The most obvious example of this younger set was the prolific Booth Tarkington of Indiana, just getting started as the century closed, and destined to command perhaps the largest audience of any midwestern writer in history.

To be sure, these are but the best known of the rural writers, and even their fame has proved all too evanescent, eclipsed as it has undeniably been by some rather basic changes in literary fashion. But they and their lesser fellows across the Midwest reached a considerable audience in the decades between 1870 and 1920, an age of novel-reading in America which demonstrated among other things an established middle-class predilection for fiction. In Illinois, besides Kirkland and Garland, there were three popular writers of note: Mary Hartwell Catherwood, the author of bucolic tales of farms and hamlets; David Ross Locke, the creator of the literary comedian "Petroleum Vesuvius Nasby" but a social novelist as well; and Francis Grierson, not so popular as the other two but by far the best stylist—an expatriate who grew to love his childhood in Illinois more and more deeply as he became further and further removed from it in time and space. His *Valley of Shadows* (1909), written in London, remains the most poignant evocation of the felt life of Lincoln's Illinois ever written. Yet this striking book is unaccountably seldom recalled or read by contemporary Illinoisans.

These artists did not constitute an Illinois school of writing. As is usually the case with groups of artists, some—such as Hamlin Garland and Joseph Kirkland—were fast friends and mutually influential, while others scarcely knew of their fellow writers' existence, despite the fact that they were all by and large writing from a commonality of materials and with similar effects. But in their autonomous ways they all self-consciously attempted to realize Garland's elusive "distinctive utterance" for the Illinois country. They would have wholeheartedly echoed Eggleston's complaint that "the manners, customs, thoughts, and feelings of New England country people filled so large a place in books, while our life, not less interesting, not less romantic ... had no place in literature." Against this invidious East-West cultural distinction they dedicated their art: they would be unabashed regionalists in literature. For the modern reader, one of the natural consequences of this regionalist aesthetic is that the Illinois novel of the nineteenth century is crammed with social history. It represents the works and days of common folk and insists upon drawing its scenes and portraits realistically, with carefully reproduced dialect, with foibles, superstitions, and peculiar mannerisms, with evangelistic religion, frontier politics and democracy and lawlessness, and with, eventually, the institution in the country towns of social class distinctions and a "higher" mode of civilization. The novelists began by assuming that the farms and towns of rural Illinois were centers of cultural value, and this important fact they wished to dramatize to a skeptical country at large. Then if America still sniffed at its westerners and their society at least the nation would know the truth about the objects it scorned.

"Let only the truth be told," was the advice Joseph Kirkland gave to novelists, and he might have been speaking for the entire tribe of midwestern writers. If the truth in question was humble, it was nonetheless the root and stalk of a mature Illinois. If the action was homely, even desultory, when compared with the traditional historical romance, was there not beauty enough in a greening field of Indian corn and drama enough in the social events attendant to the harvest to see their unpretentious art through? It is easy to see now that their preoccupation with the notion that the great American novel would spring from regional soil was both artistically naive and culturally limited. The forgotten books of Illinois regionalist authors, moldering on dusty library shelves across the state, their privacy so rarely violated, are mute testament that greatness was not the province of Illinois local color fiction. But we must ask whether this indicates a failure of art or of the particular conception of art they entertained? After all, America is a nation of regions—or was until quite recently—and regions are made up of locales ... and locales of places, some as public as a courthouse square on assizes day, some as hidden as a poor white's clapboard shack in the swampy backwater of some southern Illinois creek, or private "behind thick blinds, in dark, in woody parlors" of Queen Anne houses. The concept of local color in art ought to retain more than a passing interest for us today. The fact that these writers and their works did not completely succeed is not a sufficient reason to disregard them. It may turn out that the articulation of a culture was flawed because the culture itself was incomplete. But at any rate, the "distinctive utterance" for Illinois remains inchoate in the materials of rural life and in the novels that only partially brought artistic coherence to the land and people. It is no indictment of the regionalists to say that they have but shown later writers the way, for, in Gide's words, "without them there would be no culture." The Midwest, Illinois, Spring County—these have not yet had their William Faulkner or their Wright Morris. But one suspects that when he or she comes along some of these long-neglected books on dusty shelves in public libraries will once again be taken down and read, and that will be the beginning of the final literature of rural Illinois.

The Fictional City

The primal facts of Illinois literature, as of Illinois life, are platted farmlands and the city of Chicago. Such a potent cultural axis between country and city is perhaps not to be found in any other state, and this one has been seen by historians as definitive of the Illinois experience for over a century—or at least since the emergence of modern Chicago after the Great Fire of 1871. The popular formulaic writers who dealt with the theme of country and city tended to reduce the problem to the inane level of Virtuous Country versus Evil City, but such blatant oversimplification rarely appealed to the serious students of Illinois civilization. The better writers, such as Garland, recognized the fact that there was a healthy continuity between the urban and the rural if one took the trouble to look with unprejudiced eyes. They were genuinely charmed by this realization and used it resonantly in the best of their fiction. Garland's own *Rose of Dutcher's Coolly* (1895), for example, offers as its protagonist a woman whose girlhood and adolescence were agrarian but whose maturation depended upon a probing urban initiation into the mysteries of Chicago. This heroine was conceived as a psychically whole person, the creation of a total culture—a culture not at all polarized but rather continuous from Cairo to Chicago.

True it is, however, that not many writers tried to work with this difficult theme of integral country and city. For every rural writer who looked to the city for material there were a dozen or so who scorned the downstate area and proudly proclaimed the urbanization of their art. They were in furious competition for what Theodore Dreiser called the "laurels of laureate" of the puissant "Florence of the West" (Dreiser again) on the shores of Lake Michigan. So fascinating did Chicago prove to writers between 1880 and 1920, so beguiling as a literary subject, that some historians have spoken of a Chicago Renaissance in those years. To this one might respond: what was being reborn? Was there indeed a Chicago literature before the Great Fire of 1871? Certainly not in the sense of a social, distinctively urban literature, not to say a literature of place, one which treated the city as a city and developed an unmistakable urban landscape—the Loop, the Stockyards, the university and the southern suburbs, the realm of North Side elegance and, of course, the mighty World's Columbian Exposition—upon which to play out its myriad dramas. The intense literary activity in Chicago during this period is far better described as a kind of artistic "Great Awakening," for the progenitors of the movement lacked the classical models requisite for a renaissance (and was this fact not at once the reason for both freshness and failure?). American literature, in Chicago and all across the land, was in its process of becoming, and this was especially true for the urban novel. The Chicago writers had hard literary ground to break, though break it they emphatically did. They strove, with all the energy of their brother workers in construction, to build novel after novel, and did so as confidently as the Chicago School of Architecture threw up their "cliff-dwellings" in the Loop—the first skyscrapers to be seen in America.

It was Henry Blake Fuller who applied the metaphor of "cliff-dwellers" to the new urban Chicagoan of the 1890s. Fuller was thinking specifically of the young businessmen and professionals whom he saw as "on the make" and quite possibly awash in the economic and social dynamism of the Loop. Here was a new generation, a new subspecies of western American, the first ever to be so completely urban-bound in their lives. And the ten, eleven, even fourteen story buildings in which they worked became symbolic microcosms for the American romance of vaulting ambition and upward social mobility. When a young lawyer or physician crossed the threshold of some fictionalized Monadnock Building, walking past the tobacconist's stand and climbing into one of the newfangled elevators, he was confident of ascending in more ways than one. For Fuller and others this urban scene was another sort of literary frontier, every bit as needful of articulation as the agrarian part of the state. The radical difference in the case of the Chicago novel is its almost exact contemporaneousness with the events it describes. As Chicago grew and its urban institutions matured, a tribe of novelists and journalists immediately recorded and began turning over the facts of the city. Their eyes were sharply focused on the immense physical prospects of the town, their ears attuned to its pulsating rhythms. It is instructive simply to list some of the well-known writers who were active in Chicago during these years of burgeoning growth: Hamlin Garland, Henry Blake Fuller, Robert Herrick, Theodore Dreiser, Frank Norris, Upton Sinclair, Frank Harris, Margaret Anderson, Carl Sandburg, Harriet Monroe, Vachel Lindsay, Eugene Field, Peter Finley Dunne ("Mr. Dooley"), Sherwood Anderson, and Floyd Dell. And these are only the ones who have found their way into the academic history of American literature. Together they created in their works and lived in their professional existence a kind of cultural vortex—the beginnings of a tradition or "living chain"—which drew into it scores of lesser writers such as Mary Alice French ("Octave Thanet") and Joseph Medill Patterson, to name only two. It is a matter of historical fact that these writers, working for the most part independently, produced a body of Chicago literature, mostly novels, whose quantity is astonishing and whose quality can serve as an indication of the national health of popular writing around the turn of the century.

As might be expected, a number of these writers were not native Chicagoans. By percentage of the population there weren't many native Chicagoans in 1890, and writers were as powerfully drawn to the city as the million or so immigrants who came to its heart from the East and the South and from Europe. Moreover, some of the most successful of the Chicago writers scarcely can be said to have lived in the city at all. They were the "tourists," as Hamlin Garland termed them, the ones he thought least likely to understand the real felt life of the city and its institutions and consequently also the least likely to write the definitive Chicago novel. Yet all these Chicago writers, whether "Old Residents," adopted citizens, or just tourists, were irresistibly called to the city by the centripetal force of its culture-in-the-making. Citified or not, affirmative of urbanism or downright suspicious, they were quick to admit the literary potential of the city, and this they did without demurral—even a transplanted eastern "Mugwump" like Robert Herrick was drawn in— perceiving in Chicago the predominate urban symbol of the day, not only for Illinois and the Midwest but for the entire nation. It was Chicago rather than New York that provided the ready *mise en scène* for America's disturbing dramas of emerging proletariat and bourgeoisie. The social conflicts of the 1880s and '90s, excruciating though they were to the country, were literary godsends to writers who were thus spared the labor, unnatural to realists, of inventing their subjects. The strike at International Harvester followed by the Haymarket Riot and its bitter aftermath; the papier-mâché idealism of the Columbian Exposition, locally known as the "Fair" or the "White City," which bedazzled nearly everyone, despite its flimsiness of construction and ideology; then the horrifying depression of late 1893 and the devastating Pullman strike early the next year—these events occurred within a period of six or seven years and contained a national emotive potential that needed only artistic synthesis to become a compelling and credible version of the American urban dilemma. Because Chicago symbolized this social drama, it is not surprising that the novelists who used it in literature were less concerned with the city as place than as stage or literary setting. Their urban evocations were more those of a generalized city ambience, a symbolic landscape: a land of big buildings and even bigger events, particularized almost entirely by and through the individual characters set into action amid the urban welter. Chicago was the laboratory for the variegated experiments of the social novelists. It is safe to say that the experimenters lacked the necessary controls for their experiments, but searched no less earnestly for the sort of social generalizations that offered either order or at least the promise of order at some vague future time of urban good sense. Oddly enough, the literary treatment of Chicago as social laboratory resulted in a national aggrandizement of the city's reputation, but it also meant that a more refined and purely evocative literature of place would have to be left to their literary descendants in the later twentieth century. And the task is unfulfilled yet.

Viewed collectively, the Chicago novel of this period is a notable contribution to American literature. With the exception of some of Howells's important work, treating the same themes but using Boston and New York as representative cities, no American novelist or group of novels offers a body of urban fiction which, in artistic authority or social incisiveness, seriously rivals the work of Henry Blake Fuller, Robert Herrick, Theodore Dreiser, and Frank Norris. Indeed, it is hard to imagine a more coherent literary view of an American city being given by so many writers over so short a period of time. The temptation is great to talk about a Chicago school of novel-writing, but, as was the case with the ruralists, the similarities are much more to be found in social perspective than in artistic influence and imitation. Sad to say, almost all of this great outpouring of Chicago fiction is today unfamiliar. Only a few titles are kept alive through American literature courses in high schools and colleges around the state. One may recognize the title of Frank Norris's *The Pit* (1903) or Dreiser's *Sister Carrie*. Novels such as these are admirably instructive in the doctrines of literary naturalism and are time and again cited as examples and excerpted for anthologies. More rarely, the whole works are assigned and read. But there is so much more to this phenomenon called Chicago fiction. The many out-of-print books patiently await a contemporary readership, people who would like to gain a feeling for the crucible years of one of the world's great cities. Few questions ought to preoccupy modern Americans more than those concerning how a city matures—and grows old. Perhaps more than we realize, one of the keys to understanding a city's life cycle is to be found in the robust literature of its youth and adolescence.

Rediscovering a Tradition

The literature studied in these essays, whether country or city, agrarian or urban, is assumed to be a significant but rather sadly neglected part of the artistic heritage of Illinois—and therefore of the Midwest and America as well. The obscurity of the books which make up what I will be calling Illinois literature raises an important question, one which I feel merits the attention of both scholar and citizen: can the ethos of a state or region or nation be adequately understood if a considerable segment of its literature, though no more than a century removed in time, goes almost entirely unread? Of course, the answer I would give is an emphatic no. And a basic motivation for this study is my strongly held belief that midwestern literature of the late nineteenth and early twentieth centuries deserves to be restored to something like its former status of cultural currency and credibility. Otherwise, is it not obvious that the reasonable goal of knowing what one would like to think of as a civilization in Illinois and the great heart of the country must continue beyond the grasp of any of us—native or tourist, interested citizen or merely casual student? The creation of a culture at any time and for any society requires its re-creation from the materials of the past. And that act of re-creation, the search for a "usable past," as Van Wyck Brooks termed it, ought to be as ongoing and as serious as anything we do.

This problem of cultural wholeness is pointed up by a well-known fact about Illinois, so well known that it is in the imagination of every school boy or girl who looks at the picture on the classroom wall or opens the Illinois civics text. To think of the culture of this state is to conjure up two potent visions: first the image of virtuous homegrown statesmen (the specter of Lincoln virtually determines the political mythology of Illinois), and then the panorama of mighty social engineers, the objective-minded bankers and holders of mortgages, the town-builders and platters of land, the Chicago merchant princes and industrial kings—these are the ones who have been so glibly given the credit for having carved out a commonwealth from the wilderness. Yet if the mythos of the nineteenth century is in any sense efficacious or formative of culture today, we must see that there was incalculably more involved in the building of Illinois than these few giant figures bestriding the prairie landscape. Literature, of course, is known for its power to make manifest and to preserve the myths of a people, and within American literature surely the novel has been the most "populist" of forms. The novel is uniquely capable of delineating social class, evoking the spirit of one time or another, and dramatizing the folk beliefs which are so very determinative of national or regional character in America. More particularly, the novel dramatizes individuals within a society in ethical byplay with one another and with the concentrically circular set of communities radiating outward from their persons: for agrarian Illinois family, farm, land, and town. To the students of any society, novels offer one of the finest structural clues to the nature of the communal life of another era, a fact which is at last being discovered by historians and social scientists. But one must always remember that novels are social documents only after they have been experienced as the art they were intended to be.

Hence these essays strive not only to present neglected documents to a modern world but to provide as well an artistic calculus for reading them. They are not primarily exercises in literary criticism, but by the same token they do not hesitate to explore the mechanics of novel-writing when such an activity serves to help us know the essence and feel the power of the visions and versions of the Illinois past embodied by various authors in their various texts. The essays are structured to follow the cultural axis from country to city, downstate agrarian to Chicago urban. Each is organized around one or more key books—novels which, in senses that will be specified, either are artistically the most interesting fictions written on their subjects or best delineate the aspects of country or city with which they are concerned. For example, Joseph Kirkland's *Zury* is the key book for the section entitled "The Country" and in fact fulfills both of the characteristics just described: artistic preeminence in its class and definitive description of the culture and region it treats. "The Country" will be followed by sections on "The Town," "City and Country," and "The City," and the essays conclude with some remarks on the contemporary directions and future possibilities of Illinois literature.

One final prefatory note: if criticism is truly concerned with "resurrecting the dead" and is not to be obsessed with the handful of masterpieces which have been produced by American literature, then studies such as this one require no justification—no matter how high the incidence of failed art among their subject matter. I would like to make it clear at the outset that I come to these novels both as a critic of texts and a critic of culture, but without, I sincerely hope, the patronizing tone so often adopted by writers on "minor" books and figures. For in a very important sense the novel-makers and their fictions are to be regarded as cultural heroes, little strugglers with big ideas now forgotten by the civilization they materially helped to create. No matter how flawed the product, the makers—the Joseph Kirklands and Francis Griersons—saw the artistic prospect before them with gravity and with humility. They viewed the embodiment of Illinois culture in fiction as an ethical imperative and responded to the call with an energy and ability that were representative of their age. How well they responded must be judged by each new generation of Illinoisans. These essays ask only that the Illinois writers be given their due: a readership.

CHAPTER I

The Country

> The charming landscape which I saw this morning, is indubi-
> tably made up of some twenty or thirty farms. Miller owns
> this field, Locke that, and Manning the woodland beyond.
> But none of them owns the landscape. There is a property in
> the horizon which no man has but he whose eye can integrate
> all the parts, that is, the poet. This is the best part of these
> men's farms, yet to this their land-deeds give them no title.
>
> —Emerson, *Nature*

Landscape and Farmscape

> These are the gardens of the Desert, these
> The unshorn fields, boundless and beautiful,
> For which the speech of England has no name—
> The Prairies.
>
> —William Cullen Bryant, "The Prairies"

The essential picture of rural Illinois today is from the air. A mile above McLean County, descending to Bloomington, the land is a farmscape of rectangular geometry: square-mile sections of land enclosing soft modulations of hills, veined tracings of streams, and, early in April, dark brown fields furrowed to hypnotic effect. Receding parallels lead the eye toward a vanishing point on the distant horizon. Everything in the scene suggests a latitude, a limitless prospect of prosperity and pastoral loveliness. So the picture has been for a very long time: since the archetypal act of ordering early in the nineteenth century, when intrepid parties of government surveyors imposed a geometric regularity on the wilderness. Before long the surveyors' lines on the maps and in the plat books became boundaries and pathways, and continuity with that formative past is today attested by the network of blacktop roads running along virtually every sectional line, north and south, east and west, with only an occasional intersection that is not at right angles. Along the roads, or set back on a modest height of land, are the farmhouses themselves, with now and then an Illinois "centennial farm"—a homestead occupied by the same family for a century or more and still lending vitality and dignity to the country. Hence, despite the incursions of corporate farming and the associated technology of giganticism, it remains easy (from the air at least) to believe that nothing much has changed in Illinois over the years. The basic elements in the farmscape have endured, will endure—as close to permanent as anything in our transient civilization. For, after all, this is what one wants to believe, and nostalgia does the rest. Like the white summer haze that softens and dissolves, nostalgia gives to the hard-edged economic realities of agriculture a golden-age patina that helps convert the contemporary Illinois farmscape into a country of the mind.

Far different was the primordial Illinois landscape. To the hopeful immigrants of 1818 the modern farmscape of peace and plenty was a distant dream whose realization depended upon the systematic transformation of the prospect westward beyond the Wabash River: an astonishing inland sea of undulating prairie grasses, delightful to the senses yet troubling in its very immensity—"boundless and beautiful" at the same time. "Desert" in Bryant's parlance, passed to him through generations of literary convention, meant not a desiccated wasteland—a given section of Illinois prairie was as likely to be swampy as dry—but an utterly deserted place, as yet innocent of the American impress and revealing only the archaeological residuum of an aboriginal empire. When Bryant linked desert and garden in "The Prairies" he was embodying in a paradox what the young nation felt as an unresolved question. What was the nature of the American West? These rolling Illinois grasslands, punctuated here and there by a small stand of timber or a turbid creek, presented a scene that could be awesome or picturesque by turns. Christiana Tillson, one of the most hard-headed of the early chroniclers of Illinois, recalls the transports of a Methodist minister in 1820, who, after climbing to the top of the Mississippi bluffs above present-day Quincy, exclaimed, "Glory, glory, glory! I'm on the Mount! the Mount! I'm on the Mount of Glory!"[1] Such visions of Mt. Pisgah, along with various other millennial exultations, were not uncommonly voiced by the first immigrants. But to the extent that it was a desert the Illinois prospect was inimical both to farming and to civilization. The point, said objective-minded pioneers, was to change desert to garden. And this is what they immediately set about doing—with an energy and a will born, as some of them thought, of destiny.

Yet to romantic pilgrims like Bryant (who toured the Illinois country in 1832) the prairies were fine in their natural state, presenting a new aspect of the vast American landscape. Though nature wore in the West a different face from the cloves and cataracts of the Catskills, her call to the romantically inclined was the same: far from human institutions, in the midst of unsullied beauty, she would make men and women whole again. This was the old dream of Rousseau and Chateaubriand, and latterly of the English romantic poets, chiefly Wordsworth, of whom Bryant was a follower: a high-toned program for literature—and for literary tourists— but could it work for the immigrant? Surprisingly, some of the narratives of actual settlers are imbued with recognizably this same romanticism. One of the best of these is Eliza W. Farnham's *Life in Prairie Land* (1846), written reminiscently from the East after several years of the great pioneering experiment in Illinois. *Life in Prairie Land* is a fascinating miscellany of frontier adventures, folklore, natural history, sharply observed manners, and, stitching the otherwise amorphous mass together, a sustained and lovely hymn to the land. The romantic keynote to the book is sounded in the preface: "I have loved the West, and it still claims my preference over all the other portions of the earth. . . . it presents itself to me in the light of a strong and generous parent, whose arms are spread to extend protection, happiness, and life to throngs who seek them from other and less friendly climes. . . . If nature ever taught a lesson which the endwarfed, debased mind of man could study with profit, it is in these regions of her benignest dispensations."[2]

But what is nature to Eliza Farnham, the wild or the domesticated, the pristine landscape or the cultivated farmscape? On the one hand the purest romantic imperative calls for a "desert":

> I can never forget the thrill which the first unbounded view on a prairie gave me. I afterwards saw many more magnificent—many richer in all elements of beauty, many so extensive that this appeared a mere meadow beside them, but no other had the charm of this. I have looked upon it a thousand times since, and wished in my selfishness that it might remain unchanged, that neither buildings, fences, trees, nor living things should change its features while I live, that I might carry this first portrait of it unchanged to my grave. I see it now, its soft outline swelling against the clear eastern sky, its heaving surface pencilled with black and brown lines, its borders fringed with the naked trees (pp. 47–48).

These are the familiar aesthetics of nostalgia, with the scene delineated in precisely the picturesque sense of the word ("this first portrait ... pencilled with black and brown lines"), but the utilitarian obverse of romanticism demanded that the land be used—and not so much in the hunter-gatherer way as in the agricultural. Only then might the vast democratic and Jeffersonian promise of spiritual and social renewal (romantic in the extreme) be fulfilled for the countless yeoman farmers who were coming to take up the land.

> In less favored portions of the earth, man is more or less enslaved. Want, custom, artificial desires, or some of the thousand phantoms that tread upon the heels of human enjoyment, restrain his freedom.... Here, it is to a great extent otherwise. Our genial climate and exhaustive soil afford an abundant and ready return for his labors. He is soon released from want, and his faculties, rebounding from their depressed condition, go leisurely forth in quest of happiness.... Nature in her loveliest and benignest aspect is spread before him. She invites him to her acquaintance; and while he courts it, the jarring selfishness in which his life has been spent softens into greater harmony with the good, the true, and the beautiful in creation. He becomes a better, wiser, happier man. His fetters crumble, and he begins to reach forth to ascertain the boundaries and qualities of the new sphere in which he finds himself (p. 89).

In short, says the narrator's sister (who has been speaking from the unanswerable perspective of five formative years in the Illinois country), "Social and physical freedom exist here in their most enlarged forms" (p. 89).[3]

Such was the romantic case for Illinois. But an earlier and less susceptible traveler, while he had also found the prairies "boundless" and inviting, chose to subtitle his own eyewitness account *A Caution to Emigrants*, so unsanguine was John Stillman Wright about the new state's straggling frontier society.

> On entering Illinois I beheld a vast, and almost boundless body of land, stretching before and around me.... everything seemed to invite me to select a spot, begin my improvements, and enjoy my happy fate. But ah! like the enjoyment of forbidden pleasure, there is a sting behind. Not only is an exhorbitant price demanded, but the *inhabitants*, the people among whom I must spend my days; with whom my intimacies, my friendships are to be formed; to whom I must look for all those delicate attentions which spread a charm over

society; for an interchange of all those kind and endearing offices, so indispensably necessary in the hour of trouble and sickness: the *inhabitants*, I repeat, are sufficient to dispel the gay vision: it is impossible to dream long in a land of such palpable realities.[4]

Wright spoke frankly and for the party of the skeptics. Indeed, the advice to prospective immigrants—and both advice and immigrants were legion—was conflicting in the extreme, depending on which pamphlet one happened to read. Christiana Tillson and Eliza Farnham were both redoubtable pioneers and keen delineators of frontier mores, but they were wholly at odds about the spiritual value of the West. Here, by contrast with *Life in Prairie Land*, is Tillson's first glimpse of the Illinois prairie: "This was my first introduction to a real prairie, and I must say I was sorely disappointed. Your father had talked so much about their beauty that I expected to feel a kind of enchantment. He said, 'You never saw anything like this before.' I said, 'No'; but did not say I never saw any thing more dismal" (pp. 65–66).[5] To Tillson Illinois was mostly barrens and sloughs and dismal wasteland, on which the settlements of the vulgar inhabitants were most inauspiciously planted (she eventually retired to Massachusetts). Tillson echoes Wright, but there was always someone ready to second Farnham, too: Illinois was a "backwoods utopia" or it was a refuge for yahoos and social pariahs. The land was beautiful and amazingly fertile or it was plain and niggardly. And so the debate continued in lively fashion right up to the middle of the century.

Eventually, however, after the disaffected had gone back or gone on, a dominant viewpoint emerged. The land was good—better than the old country, where none was to be had; certainly better than the rocks and hills of New England; and even better than Ohio, if only one might find a choice tract not already occupied or in the hands of speculators. After 1815, with the British threat in the West at an end, emigration to Illinois began in earnest.[6] As new settlers quickly filled up the areas around Kaskaskia, Vandalia, and Shawneetown, the few remaining native Americans and the long-established French were displaced, their hunter-trader proclivities making it easier to move along than to oppose these strangers, who behaved as if Illinois had never been inhabited and whose possession of its prairies now seemed inexorable. The pioneers came under the imperative of the land, and, as more and more of Illinois was opened for settlement to the north and west, business became brisk at the several land offices around the state.[7]

As to the quality of the settler taking up the land, we have seen the acerbic opinion of John Stillman Wright, who retreated to New York as precipitately as possible. And even the most ardent apologists for Illinois had to admit the doubtful character of some of the immigrants. Those who had gotten in earliest to stake their claims—sometimes ahead of the surveyors—were downright suspicious of those who followed and touted the rule of law. Wasn't this law just a trick to dispossess them? Nor did this sort always respond to the communal necessities that brought frontier folk together: to raise a house or church, to fight a raging prairie fire, to bury the dead after an epidemic. Many of the early squatters were from Kentucky and Tennessee, men and women of the "kep yer distance" variety, who thought a neighbor uncomfortably close if the smoke from his dwelling could be seen from theirs. It took more than the fact of Illinois statehood to bend them to the will of the law (what it took was a band of regulators, often themselves only self-appointed ministers of justice and not legitimate agents). Like Fenimore Cooper's Ishmael Bush in *The Prairie* (1827), they had left civilization behind without regret and viewed its trappings, including the legal system, with contempt. "I have come into these districts," Bush said, "because I found the law sitting too tight upon me and am not overfond of neighbors who can't settle a dispute without troubling a justice and twelve men." Their land they held by preemption or, more often, by squatting. And they defied anyone to move them, legal right or no: "Can you tell me, stranger, where the law or reason is to be found which says that one man shall have a section, or a town, or perhaps a county to his use and another have to beg for earth to make his grave in?"[8] Ishmael Bush is of course a fictional character, but the early eyewitness narratives suggest that his type may have been more representative than we would like to think. Morris Birkbeck, an Englishman who emigrated to Illinois before statehood and did much to boost the country in his *Letters from Illinois* (1818),[9] was sensitive to the charge that the Kentuckians in Illinois were "semi-barbarians," and he tried to justify their conduct on the basis of frontier exigencies: "The first settlers, unprotected and unassisted amid dangers and difficulties, have been accustomed from early youth to rely on their own powers; and they surrender with reluctance, and only by halves, their right of defense against every aggression, even to the laws which themselves have constituted."[10] If Birkbeck meant to imply that such radical individualism was ultimately to the social good of America, it was a view vindicated near the end of the century by the historian Frederick Jackson Turner, whose now perhaps over-familiar essay "The Significance of the Frontier in American History" made a paradigm out of antisocial behavior. "The wilderness masters the colonist. It finds him a European in dress, industries, tools, modes of travel, and thought. It takes him from the railroad and puts him in the birch canoe. It strips off the garments of civilization, and arrays him in the hunting shirt and moccasin. It puts him in the log cabin of the Cherokee and the Iroquois, and runs an Indian palisade around him. Before long he has gone to planting Indian corn and plowing with a sharp stick; he shouts the war cry and takes the scalp in orthodox Indian fashion."[11]

Whatever the contemporary status of Turner's famous frontier thesis among historians—and the grandiose sweep of its central metaphor, the stripping naked before nature, is bound to disturb an age of quantifiers—it is striking that Turner hit upon the mythic narrative pattern that western novelists were already using by the 1890s and that would continue to inform the apparently inexhaustible genre of the American western for years to come. To be sure, Turner vitiated the authority of his thesis by refusing to acknowledge that some aspects of culture (memory, for example) stayed with the colonist, but the idea of sloughing off old-world ways and starting over with nature has become an important part of the American's self-regard (even now, when it is scarcely a possibility at all). In Birkbeck, Turner, and the writers who would later be called regionalists we see a powerful will to believe: the frontier is productive of individualism and democracy, just as the religion of nature is salutary for the spirit.[12] It had to be so: otherwise the violent devolution in the wilderness lacked positive social implication.

At all events the settler needed more than Turner's "sharp stick" to break the Illinois prairies! And if he took scalps, followed the patriarchal law of the clan, and accepted the expediency of the vigilance committee, before long these things too had to pass. The continuous movement of the frontier into unsettled lands carried the unreconstructed Ishmael Bush types with it. Those who stayed behind—and many did not—were generally ready to subsume the antisocial tendencies of individualism under the law. In part this concession came from a sobering recognition of what sinking roots was likely to mean in a still-isolated situation, and partly from an incipient regional pride that began to grow after statehood, a pride born of confidence in the national democracy which guaranteed liberty and in the local homestead which, when held in fee simple and tended with resolute independence, promised what western-ers universally called a competency. And no one among the committed was more enthusiastic about Illinois than Morris Birkbeck:

I *own* here a far better estate than I *rented* in England, and am already more attached to the *soil*. Here, every citizen, whether by birthright or adoption, is part of the government, identified with it, not *virtually*, but in fact.... I love this government; and thus a new sensation is excited.... I am become a patriot in my old age.[13]

The social compact here is not the confederacy of a few to reduce the many into subjection; but is indeed, and in truth, among these simple republicans, a combination of talents, moral and physical, by which the good of all is promoted in perfect accordance with individual interest. It is, in fact, a better, because a more simple state than was ever pourtrayed by an Utopian theorist.[14]

Birkbeck was at pains to show the practicability of the "fee-simple empire." His Albion on the English Prairie was not to be confused with the sort of Utopian vision that nowhere could be made to work.

Yet for others western community failed through the absence of just those virtues Birkbeck praised as manifest in the country. Even Eliza Farnham, though rhapsodic about Illinois as her spiritual home, perceptively noted the restless, rootless tendencies of the westward movement:

Liable at any moment to be pressed upon in his chosen home by eastern emigrants, the western farmer feels that he must retreat from it. He has little sympathy with the living tide that is flowing over his beautiful plains from the land of the rising sun, and when it has passed and closed around him, he feels a stranger in his own home. The charms for which he loved the country are no longer there, the spirit which bound him to it ... has fled to the untenanted plains beyond, and thither he must follow it. Of what avail then were it to build, as if his life were to be spent here? He must be ever moving, ever in the van of civilization, pressing hard upon the Indian, whose footstep brushes the first dew from the face of nature in all these magnificent kingdoms of her greatest wealth (p. 209).

This spiritualized, romantic pursuit of solitude in nature may not have been what the squatting Kentuckian or Ishamel Bush had in mind when he warned others to "kep yer distance," but the social effect was the same: moving became wandering and the prairie west was forgotten for the mountains and beyond. Thomas Hubbard was another who voiced deep doubt about the ideals of western community. He kept a remarkable journal of his experiences in Illinois in the mid-1840s (as he tried farming on the Rock River, near Dixon, in Lee County). A sensitive observer of the social scene, he was profoundly disillusioned by the lack of patriotic and communal feeling among the settlers: "There is no

Fatherland in the West & at the mention of State debts the settler shoulders his rifle & puts further west—beyond the pale of taxation—Not so at home—each man will toil & struggle to disenthrall the land that has given to himself & ancestors a home."[15] "Home" was New York State, though what he says could apply to the old world as well. Hubbard was one of the unnumbered who didn't "take" in Illinois and moved progressively westward—not to avoid a bit of tax but in search of that sense of community Americans are always looking for as they run away from its all-too-flawed embodiment in the settled areas. We hear of him in Iowa, in Kansas, but never again in New York ... or in Illinois.

His brother, Charles Hubbard, did stay. Through the years he continued to farm the land, raise a family. His own journal was of the "works and days" variety, so he missed what his introspective younger brother would surely have noticed: how gradually the elder myth of individualism gave way to a communal vision of virtuous yeomen on their bountiful farms, a persistent latter-day myth that has somehow survived every attempt at debunking. In another generation or two, after the Civil War, Illinois was looking much more like a civilization, and the people, with some hard-won leisure, began to give rein to their imaginations. The characteristic anti-intellectualism associated with pioneering softened; the "palpable realities" of which the disappointed John Stillman Wright had spoken eventually assumed heroic proportions in the collective memory of the state, kept alive by the surviving old settlers and their "filial-pietistic" biographers. After the manner of most societies, Illinoisans looked back to the stirring times of earliest settlement. There was, after the traumatic disruptions of the Civil War, a strongly felt need for a foundational cultural myth that could sustain the antinomies of the heroism of pioneering—nature was brutal—and the destiny of an agrarian empire—nature was, and is, beneficent. This was, around the turn of the century, the cardinal task of history and fiction, particularly of the new rural novel. But an intervening half-century of social and economic transformation helped make "romance" more attractive for fiction than "palpable reality," even in the work of a self-proclaimed realist such as Joseph Kirkland.

Zury—Realism and the Romance of Pioneering

When his first and best novel, *Zury: The Meanest Man in Spring County*, was published in 1887, Joseph Kirkland was fifty-seven years old, a thoroughly urbanized Chicago lawyer and an active participant in the cultural life of the city. Almost furtively, amid the welter of business and family life, he had managed a little time here and there for writing the one book that was really in him. In *Zury*, Kirkland was at last acknowledging both a family literary tradition and his own agrarian roots. For Joseph was the second generation of Kirklands to try a career in literature. His mother, Caroline Stansbury Kirkland, had written one of the best accounts of western frontier life in Michigan,[16] and the son, innocently enough, thought of himself as following in her footsteps and fulfilling the promise of of her earlier local-color experiments. While mother and son equally prized the subjects of everyday life in the West, Joseph Kirkland was convinced that the era of plain speaking was at hand. Simply by virtue of living late in the nineteenth century—beyond the Victorian pale, he hoped—he could be more realistic in his work. ("Better the last half of the nineteenth century, with its freedom of thought, speech, and action, than any age of prescription and artificiality. Thanks to Tolstoi, Daudet, Ibsen, Thomas Hardy, and the other iconoclasts, we deal no more with the unbridled vagaries of romanticism."[17]) He would tell the unadorned truth about Illinois farm life, speaking with an independence he thought his mother had been denied.

In a manuscript biography written sometime in the early 1890s (after *Zury* had gained him a measure of national attention), Kirkland was obviously pleased to see that "following thus, at an interval of forty-five years, the path marked out by his mother by her 'New Home' in 1840, he found that his life was shaping itself in the way he would have been happy, during all his career, to foresee."[18] Whomever he was trying to persuade with this, Kirkland very well knew that the "life work" of authorship was in fact a project of a few years, and rather late years at that. Writing came at the end of a long list of other experiences: boyhood in the forests of Michigan, coal-mining and railroad work in Illinois, Civil War service, and, of course, the practice of law in Chicago. We can smile at the self-aggrandizement implicit in the phrase "life work," yet no matter how long it took him to begin, Kirkland was a writer from the late 1880s until his death in 1894. In an unassuming sense, Kirkland thought of himself as the father of Illinois (and midwestern) realism, and was not above taking a hortative stance with the younger writers. One who responded positively was Hamlin Garland, with whom Kirkland struck up a firm friendship after the younger man gave *Zury* a sympathetic notice in the Boston *Evening Transcript* (16 May 1887).

At the time of the review Garland was a displaced westerner, his head full of notions gained from reading European literature and radical economics in the Boston Public Library. Reading through this surprising novel of early rural Illinois, he may have discovered some of his own inchoate ideas about western cultural greatness already in fictional form. For Kirkland was something of an original, and *Zury* was opening new, if limited, artistic territory—plenty enough to encourage those who, like Garland, would be doing their best regional writing in the coming decade. In chronicling the pioneers of Wayback, Spring County, Illinois, Kirkland was deliberately challenging the venerable eastern genteel tradition, with its dogmatic insistence on refinement. It was an example that would be followed time and again. True to his mother's spirit in *A New Home*, he was delighted to be flying democracy's banner in traditionally genteel precincts (he sent his very western book to the very eastern firm of Houghton, Mifflin). *Zury* tells of the title character's rise from the mud of Illinois bottomland to the status of country squire and state legislator, and finally to the exalted condition of marriage to a woman of cultured New England stock. It was Kirkland's pronouncement of social equality between East and West, "malodorous," he gleefully remarked, "to the cultivated and refined olfactories" of an eastern audience.[19]

Mild as it seems today, *Zury* was iconoclastic. Kirkland put his heart into its composition. He spoke of taking "infinite pains" with the novel,[20] and one feels in reading that he was for once in his life consumed by a subject: the first full-length portrait of a western American farmer, involving the dual romances of pioneering and courtship. The courtship follows a conventional comic structure, and takes up a good deal of room in the novel. But the romance of pioneering, though contained within the first five chapters, is fundamental to the book, dramatizing as it does the formative influence of nature, the wilderness, the frontier on the character of Zury Prouder—and by extension, Kirkland would say, on the western, that is, the really American, character.

The Prouder section on Illinois's Grand Paraira,[21] as they call it, quickly becomes the scene of a primal battle between colonist and nature:

> Great are the toils and terrible the hardships that go into the building up of a frontier farm; inconceivable to those who have not done the task or watched its doing. In the prairies, Nature has stored, and preserved thus far through the ages, more life-materials than she ever before amassed in the same space. It is all for man, but only for such men as can take it by courage and hold it by endurance. Many assailants are slain, many give up and fly, but he who is sufficiently brave, and strong, and faithful, and fortunate, to maintain the fight to the end, has his ample reward.[22]

Much of this is the now familiar rhetoric of social Darwinism, but the heroic tenor is unmistakable. The difficulty is that Kirkland is ambivalent about the nature of nature. On the one hand the relationship between man and nature is antagonistic, with nature showing her implacability the very first winter the Prouders are on the prairie: "They did break a little prairie that season, although it was too late to put in any crop. They called it twelve acres, but it wasn't. They thought they could get it fenced before frost, but they couldn't. They hoped for a mild winter, but it proved a severe one: for years afterward it was remembered, and in bitter jest was styled 'the year eighteen-hundred-and-froze-to death.'"[23] The family's penury is real, as are the physical shocks of an unfriendly environment. Soon baby sister dies, mother Selina turns woolly-minded, while old Ephraim becomes lazier and more dispirited than ever. And young Zury? He starts to exhibit tendencies toward the meanness that will one day be his cardinal humor. Where in all this is the Rousseauistic ideal of human perfection in nature? It takes distinct hints at a comic structure for the novel (such as the sardonic humor of the first winter's description) to keep us from expecting an unrelievedly gloomy story of arrested development and human waste in a hostile environment—along the lines of Edgar Watson Howe's tragic *Story of a Country Town* (1883). In *Zury*, however, it is the natural environment rather than the social that seems to be man's enemy: society, after all, is embryonic in Wayback City and is a couple of generations away from the stultifying provincialism later writers would associate with the small midwestern town. For Kirkland, as for Turner, nature and the wilderness are formative of character, but the heroic positivism of Turner's vision is a fraud when nature conspires to belittle man's stature in the landscape.

Yet at the same time Kirkland wants to make nature beneficent. Spring County is pictured as a natural paradise:

> Spring County is one of those highly-prized and early-sought-after localities where both prairie and timber awaited the settler. Spring River in the course of ages had dug for itself a deep ravine, through which it runs between high banks,—sometimes abutting the river in bluffs, sometimes receding from it and leaving broad bottoms.... On each bank a belt of country was then ... covered with forest primeval.... Further up the slopes, elm, oak, maple, hickory, and other hardy growths had braved and checked the prairie fires ... and prairie winds from time immemorial. Outside these timber belts, and crowding them in a stout struggle for the mastery, lies the famous "Grand Prairie." For countless years the

soil has lain fallow; crop after crop of prairie grass has grown up in summer strong and rank, and then in winter has lain down and decayed; the result of the process being a soil of great general fertility, suggestive of a thick layer of cream on a gigantic milkpan (pp. 8–9).

The image of the archetypal garden is strengthened by the description of the prairie when first seen by the awestruck Prouders:

Under the warm afternoon sun, which was already sinking in the yellow western flow of a great, cloudless sky, lay an undulating ocean of grass and flowers ... the "prairie flowers" (blue gentian) gave to the whole sward a tinge of pale azure; here and there a tall "rosin weed" would raise its spike of bloom; and again, the goldenrod gave the needed "dash of color": in damp spots there were lady-slippers and other thirsty plants; and mixed with these few examples of nature's gay moods were weeds and flowers of a thousand descriptions and as many shades of color (pp. 9–10).[24]

"This is home, is it?" Selina asks. "Wal, ferever!" (p. 11). And the narrator of the tale solemnly remarks, "Lucky the pioneer who has such woods behind him and such prairie before him at the onset of his battle with the elements" (p. 9). Again the survival rhetoric: "battle with the elements." But is this not inconsistent with the idyllic picture of a soothing, nurturing nature given in the two long passages? Whatever one wishes to call this tension between brutal and beneficent nature—inconsistency, ambivalence, or paradox—it is something neither Kirkland nor anyone else, romantic or postromantic, has been able to resolve. The battle Zury will fight is not so much to defeat nature's hostile forces as it is to find the civilizing equilibrium between nature and man. Characterizing the wilderness as a positive influence on mankind, though a romantic article of faith, goes against not only the etymology of the word but against centuries of cultural usage. For, as Roderick Nash has noted, "the wilderness was conceived as a region where a person was likely to get into a disordered, confused, or 'wild' condition. In fact, 'bewilder' comes from 'be' attached to 'wildern.' The image is that of a man in an alien environment where the civilization that normally orders and controls his life is absent."[25] Perhaps Kirkland's fictional program involves an initial battle to transform the wildest in the wilderness. In this struggle the fittest survive and come into a new harmony with nature—now ready after these feats of elemental heroism to offer her "ample reward" of "life-materials" to man. In such a program, "Wilderness and civilization become antipodal influences which combine in varying proportions to determine the character of an area. In the middle portions of the spectrum is the rural or pastoral environment (the ploughed) that represents a balance of the forces of nature and man."[26] This is what Leo Marx has called the "middle landscape" between pristine nature and pervasive urbanization,[27] but the term *farmscape* used in this essay is synonymous with both *pastoral* and *middle landscape*. The creation of the farmscape, then, becomes the dramatic task of Zury Prouder.

"Frontier life was what he needed to grow in," Kirkland says, but it is necessary to ask what sort of growth is involved. While still a boy, Zury shows a stubborn independence that will later harden into the peculiar mettle of the lonely, hard-put farmer who, from long experience of doing things by and for himself, comes to disdain community except insofar as he can use it. "One of the ways in which he showed his enjoyment of the consciousness of power was a natural impatience of control or interference, a brusque self-assertion, a rudeness which in a weaker being would have been intolerable" (p. 16). The theme of "might makes right"—Zury is justified in walking over "lesser beings" because he is powerful, survival is the issue, and Darwinian natural selection is operating—is found throughout the early chapters of the novel. Zury is naturally "nails," and he does survive where so many perish or return East. But there is a human price to pay. After the death of his little sister, Zury "settled down into a stony hardness." There was no more time for being a boy: in the face of his father's shiftlessness and his mother's incapacity, Zury became the farmer in the family, the single human will holding off the newly claimed land's reversion to wilderness.

Given a large canvas, this has the makings of a frontier saga, with Zury a kind of Anglo-Saxon Per Hansa. But then Zury is *mean*, mean as any miser in literature. Having learned all too early about buying low and selling high, Zury, untutored and unchecked, simply gets worse as he gets older. Swimming the river to avoid paying ferriage might have made some sense in the early days, when money was scarce, but in a few years parsimony ceases to be a virtue and becomes a comic vice. In the initial years on the Grand Prairie, Kirkland tells us, the need for money "made a deep impression on the forming mind of the youth; and being of a logical turn, he 'put this and that together,' and drew conclusions fitted to the premises as he saw them. Money was life; the absence of money was death. 'All that a man hath will he give for his life; *ergo* all a man hath will he give for money'" (p. 30). It is a skewed but highly symbolic syllogism, yoking as it does the American's spiritual welfare to the wild horses of his material progress, in a coupling that has endured. The novel uses survival to rationalize the christening "Usury." Old Ephraim Prouder, though unable to strike the mark himself, has yet the satisfaction of seeing his Usury surpass all parental expectations—a competency and considerably more. But what of the human broadening and mellowing that are supposed to come with material sufficiency? And what of love? Not bartering in the commodity of a wife ("And so Mary went to work for Zury very much as Jule [the black hired man] did, only it was for less wages" [p. 85]), but *love?* Of course, these things are far harder to attain than a competency, for—and this is the major thrust of the novel's comic irony—they are the very ones the hardened Illinois farmer, from brutalizing toil and isolation, is inured against. In short, Zury can make no spiritual progress until he overcomes his meanness, the same meanness that kept him alive and eventually gave him the leisure to ask what is perhaps the first civilized question: what is life for?

The moral rehabilitation of Zury Prouder is the central concern of the courtship plot, which is itself an odd mixture of comedy and melodrama, psychological realism and sentimentality. Initially Anne Sparrow, who is the impoverished daughter of a New England clergyman and has come to Wayback as a schoolmarm, finds Zury odious because of his brutish manners and his meanness; for his part, Zury is intimidated both by Anne's cultural attainments and her staunch independence (he is also married). Near the middle of the novel, however, Anne convinces Zury to act the part of John Alden (she is Priscilla) in an amateur theatrical. This causes a sensation among the gone-to-seed Puritans of Wayback, and when it is learned that Zury's wife (who is conveniently absent) has died, there is whispering that the hand of Providence is in it and that the stage marriage of John and Priscilla is a literal joining of Zury and Anne. As if this were not enough, Zury and Anne are forced by a prairie fire to take refuge for the night in an abandoned coal mine; Zury, recognizing the impropriety, wants to go for help, but Anne—who has a phobia about darkness—won't hear of his leaving. In a state of hysteria she clings to Zury, they have sexual intercourse, and Anne becomes pregnant.

In the light of day Anne is revolted, Zury scared. She fears loss of respectability; he is afraid of extortion, or worse, of marriage to Anne, meaning sharing of wealth (she actually has no intention of doing either). Facing ostracism from the community, Anne is ready to return to the East, until her life's savings are lost in a fire set by a mob. Now utterly helpless and desperate lest her pregnancy become known, Anne, with Zury's help, arranges a marriage to a long-standing and innocent suitor,

John McVey. Zury, who despite his meanness cannot refuse, sets John up in business, and Anne's character is saved, though she certainly feels nothing like love for the foolish McVey. For the twins soon born to her, however, she feels an immense affection and determines to devote the rest of her life to their rearing. But a few years later John McVey gets the gold fever and rushes off to California, where he conveniently dies of the cholera and is immediately forgotten by everyone at Wayback. This removes the last situational obstacle to Zury and Anne coming together (Zury's second wife has also died!), and sets the stage for Zury's reform and Anne's acceptance of him.

Many of these events appear ridiculous in a synopsis: in context they are often enlivened by comic dialect and a pervasive good humor (this cannot be said of Anne's morbidity, which is discussed below). By the time Zury is persuaded to run for the legislature, the comic denouement is in sight. From the outset the novel has stressed his honesty:

> "Th' ain't nothin' *mean* abaout Zury, *mean* 's he is. Gimme a man as sez right aout 'look aout fer yerself,' 'n' I kin git along with him. It's these h'yer sneakin' fellers th't's one thing afore yer face 'n' another behind yer back th't I can't abide. Take ye by th' beard with one hand 'n' smite ye under th' fifth rib with t'other! He pays his way 'n' dooz's he 'grees every time. When he buys 'taters o' me, I'd jest 's live 's hev him measure 'em 's measure 'em myself with him a-lookin' on. He knows haow t' trade, 'n' ef yew don't, he don't want ye t' trade with him, that's all; ner t' grumble if ye git holt o' the hot eend o' th' poker arter he's give ye fair notice. Better be shaved with a sharp razor than a dull one" (p. 86).

The meanness may be, as Kirkland says, a "dominant mania," but there is no disputing that Zury has the respect of his community, the Illinois frontier settlement, no matter how appalling his "brutal greed" might be to a New England schoolmarm. Wayback trusts Zury and looks to him for leadership, and it is inevitable that sooner or later he be sent to Springfield to represent his district.

By that time Zury has long been both the richest and meanest man in Spring County, and when he goes electioneering (with the help of Anne as speechwriter) his politics are warmly partisan—as whose were not in Illinois in the 1840s?—but not in the sense of reflexively following a party line. He is neither Whig nor Democrat, but mindful of his own interests (which he assumes to be identical with those of his constituents, since he is the most successful among them). While "whole hog" on the banking question, pleasing the Democrats and assuring that his considerable fortune will not be deflated by a flood of paper money, he is downright abolitionist on the slavery issue, speaking out freely in the face of pockets of southern sympathy around Wayback. Zury's political honesty and his antislavery principles are happy surprises to Anne, whose Yankee conscience approves of both and allows a general rapprochement between them. And once in Springfield Zury has ample opportunity to prove that Anne's new respect is not misplaced.

Kirkland was a social historian as well as a novelist,[28] and his picture of the flush times of the Illinois legislature is ironic but essentially accurate.[29] Zury at first is derided as a hayseed; his maiden speech, in comic dialect, is ignominiously hooted down ("Mr. Speaker: I dunno 's givin' a name tew a c'mitty putts any fence 'raound sech c'mitty ..." [p. 400]). Throughout it all Kirkland shows Zury to be as tough-skinned as ever, and employs a deft satirical touch to remind us that his protagonist is a better man than the average run of Illinois legislator:

> Zury had attended church conferences. He had also attended town-meetings. The General Assembly of the State of Illinois did not resemble a church conference: what it was like was a prolonged, exaggerated, disorderly town-meeting.
>
> An army of spittoons, each serving as the mere pretense of a target for tobacco-juice; an army of wire-woven waste-baskets jammed with the detritus of inchoate legislation; an army of desks whereof the chief office was the upholding of an army of boots, over the tops of which an army of politicians could insolently disregard their business and defy order and public decency. Such was the Illinois legislature *in those days* (p. 397).

"The more things change ..." Kirkland is saying, in voice with political satirists of every age, but the effect is to make Zury more palatable to the reader (his meanness has in no way diminished) and at the same time to draw out his comic comeuppance. While the real power-brokering goes on around him, Zury, the consummate horse trader, languishes in the Library and Geology and Science committees. Yet the day comes when the assembly is to elect a United States senator (as was done in those pre-Progressive days). Zury, though mightily rushed by both parties, determines to vote for a disinterested third candidate, "for a man I think fit," he tells Anne, "who hasn't offered me anything, directly or indirectly, and who wouldn't put me in a place I was not fit for, not if I could make him president!" (p. 418). (Notice the absence of dialect in this highly principled statement.) We see that Zury never cheats, only trades—and only things that mutually have value. As in farming, so in politics.

And as in politics, he assumed, so in love. Disastrous reasoning again! For Anne Sparrow McVey can no more be bought in middle age than she could as a girl. The lessons of thirty years ought to have made this obvious to Zury, but his mania has given him an apparently permanent blind spot to the fact that Anne's affections may not be traded for, try as he may with his amusing powers of insinuation: "This is going to be a trememjous country in the next generation or two, or three. Such glories as the Queen of Sheba never dreamed of, and didn't see at Soloman's court neither. A man or a woman that starts in with a hundred thousand when I drop it, will be cuttin' a broad swath before he dies. . . . Somehow, I like to think of Philip—your son—just *spreadin'* himself, after you and I are dead and gone, backed by—well, maybe a *million of money!*" (p. 426).

As a material prophecy about Ilinois and America in the second half of the nineteenth century, this could hardly be bettered. But as a proposal of marriage it is utterly mendacious and confirms Zury's position in the comic tradition of foolish old men pursuing women with invitations to wealth and status. Kirkland, however, has something that takes Zury beyond his stereotype by redeeming him through a series of self-discoveries prompted by Anne's obstinate refusal to have him so long as he remains a skinflint: "Never till now had he felt the weakness of wealth as a means of happiness. He took out the fat pocketbook, full of money and promissory notes and securities, and tried to re-awaken the spell which it ought to exercise over his sinking spirit. Vain, vain, vain! There was no joy in it at that moment. He even threw it down and trod on it! 'Ye beastly varmint! It's you that's ruined me! It's you that's made me such a———that she can't bear me, rich as I am!'" (p. 437).

In an ensuing night of agony Kirkland dramatizes the fact that even miserly, becalloused Illinois farmers may have their epiphanies. It was a lesson he learned from the English novelists of character, especially Thomas Hardy.[30] There is sensibility in this commoner, plenty enough to feel the full pain of humiliation and begin the process of regeneration.

In the darkest hour Zury cries "Oh Mother! mother!" and is taken "away back to the helplessness of childhood" (p. 438). Now comes the long overdue recognition that those early patterns on the frontier farm have been determinative. So very many lost opportunities, precluded by meanness, now parade before him in open mockery. The enormity of his spiritual desolation is finally made plain. Zury is convinced that Anne will never accept him, but the moral imperative to rid himself of his meanness and make amends is nonetheless strong: the decision to do so is his first selfless act and the first act of a new self.

To make a long story short—and *Zury* is a long story—the meanest man does in the end manage to change his ways, and concomitantly his suit with Anne starts to prosper. For weeks he makes no attempt to buy her off, instead devoting himself to her service, taking her to visit her son (actually their son) Philip, now a railroad engineer, and keeping his buckboard and team constantly at her command. "Anne, on her part, was sorely troubled in conscience, from time to time, by the thought that she was not rendering 'value received' for the faithful attentions of her elderly admirer; especially his kind considerateness in not now urging the suit which it would seem so hard and cruel and ungrateful in her to refuse" (p. 484). Now it is Anne thinking in the mercantile idiom, while Zury shows a new kind of humanized shrewdness in holding back. Surely, our comic expectations tell us, the time for marriage is near. Both principals have come a long way since their youthful conflicts: she the pert, independent eastern schoolmarm; he the self-made country squire on the school board. But age has had its predictable softening influence. The sins and disappointments of youth have been duly considered and paid for over time, and late in the day the decision is made to seize what's left of it and affirm that life—Illinois life—has after all not been in vain. Not surprisingly, Zury's final proposal bears no resemblance to any of the others: "Don't ye go to send me off again, Miss McVey—don't do it! It 'most killed me before. Young folks can turn from one thing to another, but old folks—I know I'm rough, and ignor'nt, and no gentleman, and all that; but I hain't forgot how to learn" (p. 501). She accedes, and both are winners: he has captured the East; she has changed him and will continue to supervise his civilization. He had come close to ruling her by her instincts, but the victory of culture over pioneer hardihood belongs to her. As the novel ends, a few years after Anne and Zury marry, the Prouders are busy preparing for, of all things, a grand tour of Europe. "Wal, ferever," as Selina would have said.

Anne Sparrow deserves a few words independent of Zury. She comes West, as we have seen, from economic necessity. But otherwise Anne is wholly unrelated to the Christian sisterhood of schoolmarms doing good out West—a staple of sentimental fiction before the Civil War.[31] Kirkland makes her an odd mixture of independence and frailty. Far from being a conventional Christian, Anne is depicted as a radical feminist, a convert to Fourierism, and an erstwhile member of Brook Farm:

> The whole story of the New England "socialistic movement" has never been told, and probably never will be; certainly not until the

generation of its actors shall have passed away. The annals of Brook Farm give only the surface of events. As to Anne's part, we need not inquire how far from the beaten track her "broad views" led her. Whatever she did was not done from wickedness; it was in accordance with her honest opinions of right and wrong, and not in violation of them. Her lips are sealed; she had neither praise nor blame to bestow on her former friends at the time when she begins to be connected with our story (p. 92).

Such self-conscious discretion is, of course, tantamount to titillation, and Kirkland wants us to know that Anne came to Wayback on the run from a past. "Whatever she did" apparently included concubinage (pp. 145, 169),[32] but in any case the implication of a free love creed for the young Anne Sparrow is strong. This combination of dubious religious principles (she may even be a Unitarian!), socialism, and female emancipation extending to sexual behavior was bound to get her into difficulty with the provincials of Wayback, and was almost as hard for Kirkland's audience to swallow in 1887.

The obverse of all Anne's admirable independence is her morbid fear of darkness. Regardless of the pathology of the case—and Kirkland psychologizes at length about it—Anne's phobia is a dramatic necessity in the novel, since it makes possible the fatality with which she and Zury come together in the coal mine. At times Anne is the clinging vine of the sentimental tradition—"I am alone in the world—quite alone—all alone" (p. 222), but a few paragraphs later her fear is indisputably real: "Insanity gibed and gibbered at her" (p. 223). "In her piteous plight she was suddenly seized with the boldness, the cunning, and the recklessness of desperation" (p. 222). The best interpretation of the coal-mine scene is that it is not a "tear-jerking rape-seduction" melodrama—Anne is not taken advantage of and she does not merely swoon into Zury's waiting arms—but rather a case of Anne's saving herself from madness in the only way she can. "For his nineteenth-century readers, it is a shockingly unconventional stand that Kirkland is insisting upon: there may be circumstances, he is saying, when an unmarried woman may have sexual intercourse without damage to her virtue."[33] Among those readers who saw through Kirkland's indirection to the truth of the scene, there were those who predictably cried, "Immoral!" And Kirkland, for all his devotion to telling the truth in fiction, reacted defensively. He immediately set about revising the scene (against the possibility of a second edition), but fortunately for the structural integrity of *Zury* he left the fact of Zury's and Anne's intercourse undisturbed.[34]

For the rest, Anne is as shrewd in her way as Zury in his. She never quits trying to bring culture to Wayback and achieves through perseverance, fortitude, and cleverness a marked success with her pupils. Kirkland's heroine is a distinct advance over previous western types. She is drawn larger and more boldly; she is freer and less intimidated by the role-binding concept of woman found in the settlements. She is, in fact, a sensitive and intellectual woman, though far too little is made of this in the last parts of the novel. Anne bravely puts herself into conflict with her adopted community, for she firmly believes she has something to offer which is superior to the ignorance and anti-intellectualism she finds on the frontier. She helps an embryonic society toward maturity—no pioneer, regardless of the number of acres he entered and planted, could have done more.

Zury can be taken as representative of something basic about the rural literature of Illinois and the Midwest. What the novel helped initiate for Illinois was a localized process of myth-making, the romantic recollection of an agricultural empire in its infancy, charged with heroism on the part of pioneers who are yet "just folks." Their accomplishments, real or imagined, had for the late nineteenth century the poignancy of the irrevocable, and Kirkland must surely have felt this as he struggled to re-create Spring County amid the modern urban rhythms of Chicago. At the end of his labor he took a last look at the Prouder homestead and saw with satisfaction that, over a period of more than forty years, the farmscape had marvelously evolved from idea to bountiful reality: "When we first saw it, it was the abode of toil and hardship—poor in money, comfort, grace, gayety, leisure, cultivation, refinement, liberality. Now (though so many years later, yet still in the same man's lifetime) all these things have grown and clustered about it like flowers and fruits about a lonely rock. Nature's prodigal soil and man's prodigal labor have worked ... to make a lovely island where was before a pathless waste" (p. 509).

"In the same man's lifetime ..."—so quickly had it come to pass, yet so utterly it now lay behind. A few years after the appearance of *Zury*, Frederick Jackson Turner stood before the American Historical Association at the World's Columbian Exposition in Chicago and declared that the American frontier was closed: "Four centuries from the discovery of America, at the end of a hundred years of life under the Constitution, the frontier has gone, and with its going has closed the first period in American history."[35] Joseph Kirkland may even have heard Turner's speech, and if he did he noticed its elegiac quality: from the Ohio Valley and the Old Northwest to the Pacific the frontier was gone, the way back to places like early Illinois closed forever, except to the national memory and the imagination of the artist. We can see now that it took a richly imagined Spring County to keep emotional ties with the Illinois past alive and that the continuance of those ties is not something to be taken for granted. Every so often *Zury* is rediscovered and brought back from the verge of final obscurity. But, sadly, the novel is once again out of print, and it is hard to find *any* edition to read. Ought we to have landmarks other than buildings and statues? Is there such a thing as literary preservation?

Francis Grierson's Mystical Landscape

> Out of the West come the signs and symbols of a great revival.
>
> —Grierson, *The Celtic Temperament*

There is a forgotten book about early Illinois that takes up where *Zury* leaves off—the 1850s. At its narrative core is the proposition that the locale around Sangamon County was the epicenter of an apocalypse. The notion has a built-in incredulity. What is *an* apocalypse? Accustomed as Americans are to looking for *the* Apocalypse, we are unprepared to find it in central Illinois and spelled with a lowercase *a*. Yet this is what Francis Grierson's *The Valley of Shadows* (1909) says, dramatically and convincingly. Grierson is usually remembered as that "strange fish" of an expatriate (the epithet is Van Wyck Brooks's), the son of emigrant British parents, who, after boyhood on the Illinois prairie, left the country further and further behind in a cosmopolitan career abroad as a pianist and a writer of notable personal essays. Little in his life and work suggests an emotional debt to frontier Illinois, but when Grierson, late in life, began writing *The Valley of Shadows* at his English residence, he found composition to be a labor of artistic love and exactitude. The book became a tribute to the peculiar greatness of the Illinois prairie, long ago sensed by the boy and now remembered and amplified by the man—the "great silences," as Grierson called them, which evoked the voices of preacher and prophet and Lincoln himself. The author was a mystic,[36] somewhat in the mold of Walt Whitman, and the persona of the child on the prairies was the romantic father of the man in just the platonic Wordsworthian sense. For the boy Francis had indeed been the medium through which the cathartic forces of the 1850s were being conducted to the man Grierson a half-century after.

The Valley of Shadows structures its Illinois materials around images and symbols. Social history, so prevalent in the realism of *Zury*, is de-emphasized, and there is nothing we would recognize as a sequential plot (Grierson disclaims any fictional intention). In fact Grierson found the entire philosophy of realism unpalatable: "The realistic novel can be produced by one or more persons in every town. The facts are there before you—marriages, births, divorces, feasts, and funerals; knead them, like dough for a dumpling, season the lump with the spice of passion, and the crude mass, sodden and indigestible, is ready for the market."[37] This was a strong reaction against the realism of Howells, dominant in turn-of-the-century American literature, with its championing of the great American average. Such writing, Grierson insisted, never got below the surface to the essence of things, especially to the essence of human beauty and value. But it would be a mistake to conclude from this that Grierson rejected the homely facts of rural Illinois life. On the contrary, he was convinced of their importance, but wished to go beyond social history in search of poetry. Hence the crucial role of archetypes in *The Valley of Shadows:* the garden, the apocalypse, and even Lincoln. They are part of what one might call a mystical landscape, a place where, as Grierson says, "it seemed as if anything might happen."[38]

The sense of place in literature depends on a heightened consciousness of environment and on the transactions of that consciousness with nature and man's "natural" institutions of home and garden. These Grierson innerves and imbues with metaphysical meaning. The opening Proem offers the theme that will recur throughout the narrative like a leitmotif: "It was impossible to tell what a day might bring forth." And he continues, "Thousands labored on in silence; thousands were acting under an imperative, spiritual impulse without knowing it; the whole country round about Springfield was being illuminated by the genius of one man, Abraham Lincoln" (p. 30). Here is the mystical trinity of Great Man, Great Times, and, ubiquitous and enduring, Great Nature. The confluence of the three "round about Springfield" in the 1850s transformed the area in Grierson's eyes into the mythic center of America. (His attitude in this regard happens to correspond to a secretly cherished belief of many Americans who so reverentially study Lincoln's era today).

"Never was there more romance in a new country," Grierson maintained, and he remembered himself as one of the boys "dressed in butter-nut jeans ... swinging idly on a gate," and waiting expectantly for the "great changes" everyone in Illinois anticipated. While he waited he soaked up the felt life around him, felt life he now fashioned into a series of western American genre scenes: log-cabin meeting houses lifted nigh off their crude foundations by sweet simple hymn-singing; open-air camp meetings in all their social complexity; the glory and mystery of plowing and planting, with the boy following the oxen the livelong day and never wearying (or so he remembered); the Underground Railroad, full of heroic and righteous intrigue; and, towering over the rest, the final Lincoln-Douglas debate in Alton, viewed close-up by the boy and drawn by Grierson in a monumental manner suggestive of the Missouri genre painter George Caleb Bingham.[39] All this was revelation to the English pioneer boy. And it remained fresh fifty years later.

The Valley of Shadows opens at the time of Donati's great comet,[40] its eerie tripartite tail dominating the evening sky and insinuating into the conditioned imaginations of the Illinois folk a cardinal portent of the last things. Perhaps some of them looked upon the comet with the failed millenarianism of the 1840s in mind, the recollected image of the Millerite faithful gathered on hilltops across the Ohio Valley awaiting an end that never came. But was this not merely a postponement of the inevitable? Azariah James, the local Methodist preacher, is eager to extrapolate from the sign of the comet and the recent earthquake to the imminence of the Apocalypse: "No, brethering, the Lord hez passed the time when he shakes yer cornfields en yer haystacks by a leetle puff o'wind. He hez opened the roof o' Heaven so ye can all see what's a-comin'. He hez made it so all o' ye, 'cept them thet's blind, kin say truly, '*I hav seen it.*' Under ye the yearth hez been shuck, over ye the stars air beginnin' te shift en wander. A besom of destruction 'll overtake them thet's on the wrong side in this here fight" (p. 40).

The fight is of course the approaching Civil War and the moral division over the slavery question. Rev. James threatens the proslavery members of his congregation with dark hints of divine retribution, while outside the meetinghouse—which the boy thinks of as "possessing a sort of soul"—spring is triumphant, making "of the desolate little meetinghouse and its surroundings a place that resembled a second Garden of Eden" (p. 33). The apocalyptic message within seems harshly at odds with the beautiful garden without, and this is a tension sustained during the following chapters. The country preacher's shrill pronouncement that the Day of the Besom is at hand, and Abraham Lincoln is to be its wielder, sends what Grierson calls "an electrical thrill" through the flock and gives them plenty to reflect upon as they return to their work in the Illinois garden. From that day they will scan the landscape for further eschatological portents and look forward to the regional camp meeting in the fall.

Meanwhile the English immigrants have their homestead to occupy them. For young Francis the routine of plowing and planting was the most romantic of transactions with nature. "It was like some rare holiday, a festival, a celebration"—in other words, the antithesis of the travails of the Prouder family. "All Nature seemed to partake of the joy; a new world of marvels seemed to be on the eve of consummation. The weather was perfect and as we three—my father, one of my sisters, and myself—went forth with a sack of seed, we dropped the large golden grains into the proper places all along through the soft, dark loam, closing up each hole, keeping up a ceaseless chatter ... about the pure delights of the work we were doing."

Farming, to Grierson's mind, was a "climax," a "consummation," and a "celebration," not at all resembling the elemental battle Zury's family fought in the same locale. The emotional importance of the experience is evident when the elderly man writing in London speaks right through the persona of the boy: "Perhaps never since have I felt the same kind of thrill. There are days that shine out like great white jewels in the crown of life" (p. 105). Both style and substance indicate Grierson's sense of the sacramental structure of man in nature, a paramount concept in romanticism, derived not only from Wordsworth but from Emerson as well. In *The Valley of Shadows* the farmscape is not to be carved out of nature, as in *Zury*, through a tenacious, protracted, debilitating conflict. Its creation comes from the realization in the mind of man that farm and garden are identical ("everything grew as if by nature"), or, to put it another way, from the marriage of the pioneer with a nature "feminine and dynamic, propelling all things."[41]

In this Grierson is linked with early nineteenth-century romanticism—the romanticism of Wordsworth and Schiller, to be sure, but also of Thomas Cole's landscapes and Emerson's *Nature*. Yet in another sense he is forward-looking, postromantic: the use of time and the arcing of memory over its spans. The Log-House chapter shows the boy imagining the builders and first occupants of his dwelling (the Griersons were the second occupants), some twenty-five years before the epiphanic year of 1858. Standing bedazzled among the flowers, the boy envisions the original inhabitants, while synchronically the man ponders the persona he has invented: from 1909 back to 1838, the major fraction of a century recapitulating an entire cycle of Illinois history, from genesis to senescence, with 1858 as the center. As Grierson looks through the boy's eyes with a kind of platonic astigmatism, so consonant with viewing nature both as emblematic and in flux, the narrative moves from "signs and tokens" of the Log-House's builders, to a description of the flowers around the yard, and finally to a moving account of the interior—not to speak of its rude decor or its life bustle, as would predictably be the case in most western genre writing or painting, but to isolate what Grierson calls the "residuum" of the past still palpable in the workaday present.

The boy instinctively feels that it was a woman who first planted the flower garden, and he intuits a law of correspondence between them: "Perhaps there is a secret and invisible agreement between certain persons and places" (p. 53). He imagines a woman of great natural gifts (she may even be intended as a personification of nature, since the phrase "everything grew as if by nature" refers to her garden), whose handiwork continues in the present to keep everything round the cabin in bloom—and nothing more beautifully than the morning glories, "like a living vision," enfolding the Log-House in a "canopy of infinite and indescribable colour."

> How the spell of their magic changed the appearance of the house! The flowers looked out on sky and plain with meek, mauve-tinted eyes, after having absorbed all the amaranth of a cloudless night, the aureole of early morning, and a something, I know not what, that belongs to dreams and distance wafted on waves of colour from far-away places. At times the flowers imparted to the rugged logs the semblance of a funeral-pyre, their beauty suggesting the mournful pomp of some martyr-queen, with pale, wondering eyes, awaiting the torch in a pallium of purple. They gave to the entrance a sort of halo that symbolised the eternal residuum of all things mortal and visible (p. 54).

Even granting Grierson's mysticism, this passage is dense with imagery, all centering on the color of purple and keyed by the phrase "all the amaranth of a cloudless night." Amaranth is a species of wildflower or weed with tiny purple blossoms. This meaning strengthens the sense of the homely and natural in the garden, while also recalling the idea of the unknown foundress' hand so well concealed that her work and nature's are indistinguishable in the landscape. Moreover, it fits nicely with the image (given a few paragraphs earlier) of the lowly jimsonweed standing undespised among the lilacs and sweet williams. Amaranth is also the poetic flower that never fades, an imaginative ideal whose consonance with the mystical landscape is clear. Finally, there is the amaranthine color, a sky-dark purple which the morning glories have absorbed from the "cloudless night" and are now giving forth in the light of day, along with the "aureole of early morning" and the ineffable "something" from the realm of dreams. The color reaches its ultimate intensity in the "halo" around the entrance. It is made to seem a kind of cosmic gateway, a shimmering portal into the world of forms and no longer just a rude door to a ruder cabin.

The pattern of purple imagery continues in the surprising metaphor of the flowers as "martyr-queen" and the cabin as "funeral-pyre." Awaiting immolation with "pale, wondering eyes," the queen wears a "pallium of purple," not only the requisite color of royalty but a cloak of death, a pall, both a dilation of this new theme of death and a last iteration of the dominant color image of purple. The suggestion of death's presence in this special and beautiful place is almost too unexpected even to be felt as elegiac—the ineluctable appearance of death in Arcadia that inspires not fear but melancholy: *Et in Arcadia ego.*[42] Assuming that Grierson knew what he was doing, and was not merely carried away by his poetic enthusiasm, we can suppose he intended a symbolic connection, however tenuous and indirect, between this passage and the larger theme of Illinois garden and apocalypse. For the question is bound to arise: why, if Illinos is Edenic, a natural paradise where man and the land are in harmony, is the supernatural and violent cleansing of the apocalypse necessary? The answer, fundamentally grounded in the Fall, is that the evil of proslavery thinking threatens to ruin the agrarian commonwealth (a version of the doctrine that "every prospect pleases and only man is vile"). Significantly, it is the relatively uncorrupted boy who is closest to the land, as we have seen, and whose views on the crucial issue of slavery have been conditioned by the humanitarianism of his English father (the entire family cooperates with the Underground Railroad and resolutely faces personal danger several times). Others have more reason to worry: "Fer they shell *cry* unto the Lord bekase of the oppressors, en he shell send them a savior, en a *great* one" (p. 41), shouts Rev. James, thinking of the Second Coming of Christ and the first coming of Lincoln as the same event.

And the intensifying spiritual forces are given a local focus through the highly receptive imagination of the boy. At night in the Log-House there is an "immense and immeasurable sadness"; the tolling of the wall clock fills the boy's heart "with a sense of the hollowness of things, the futility of effort, a consciousness of days and nights continually departing.... About midnight the stillness became an obsession. All Nature was steeped in an atmosphere of palpable quiet, teeming with dismal uncertainty and sombre forebodings.... The doleful duets of the katy-dids often came to a sudden stop, and during the hush it seemed as if anything might happen" (pp. 55–56). What can relieve this hour of dread? Where is the hope necessary for reaffirmation to spring from?

Grierson's answer is direct and moving. "At times streaks of cold light from the semi-circling moon would fall through the window on the old rag-carpet." Not a piece of oriental luxury nor even an Axminster such as would grace the Illinois parlors of later generations, but a make-do of rags and tatters. Yet the boy gazes raptly upon it, in search of an obscure figure—in this case more of a patchwork abstraction with its message hidden in an acrostic not easily solved. Somewhere in that carpet, he knows (and not for the first time does the old man in London make him precocious), is the clue to continuity between past and present:

> I would sit and count the pieces and compare one colour with another, for each seemed imbued with a personality of its own. Here, in the common sitting-room filled with chimeras about to vanish, each strip of cloth was a pillow for some dead thing of the past, some greeting or regret. There were strips worn when the wearer set sail from the old country, others had faced a hail of bullets at Buena Vista, passed through an Indian rising, or the first stormy meetings of the Abolitionists in Illinois (p. 57).

The reminder of the tradition of abolitionism in Illinois is timely, for its consummation is soon to come and its authority reaches even into the living room of the cabin. Separately and together, the cloth strips of the rag carpet "humanised the interior as graves humanise a plot of earth.... the rag-carpet was made for the Log-House, and the Log-House was made for man" (p. 57). After a fearful midnight vigil, reestablishment of continuity with the past brings the narrative back to the image of the foundress in her garden, instituting the western way of life through the act of planting the morning glories which will eventually transform the rugged facade of the Log-House into a transcendental gateway. Nature, death, and the humanized past—elements in the mystical landscape—combine to generate a heightened sense of place. Behind the transcendental vision is simply a western genre scene, one of literally dozens concerned with log cabins on the American frontier. Grierson's mysticism provides the alembic through which the ample sentiment and the felt life of the folk, along with the homely physical facts of their existence, are distilled into "the eternal residuum of all things mortal and visible." It is indeed genre, but genre remodeled for the highest uses of romantic rather than realistic art.

The Log-House chapter is a pastoral interlude between the initial prophecy of the apocalypse and its fulfillment at the camp meeting. In Grierson's hands the camp meeting becomes a fascinating social microcosm. This was the social history approach taken thirty-five years earlier by Edward Eggleston in *The Circuit Rider* (1874). Eggleston had seen the Methodist camp meeting as a triumph of democracy over class-feeling in the West, and he had dramatized this to fine effect, while giving his genre piece the appropriate landscape trappings of open-air and forest (for the analogue in painting, see Worthington Whittridge's *Camp Meeting*, also done in 1874). But once again Grierson goes beyond social genre in his insistence on a larger meaning to the camp meeting. The gathering in *The Valley of Shadows* is huge: thousands, rather than hundreds, attend, and its spiritual struggles extend over many days. The Illinois people are moved to leave their farms and villages deserted; they come from half a dozen neighboring counties and cannot precisely say what their motivation is, though all sense that politics and religion are being fused by the issue of slavery. "Summow, right er wrong, the people hev an idee that this here meetin' ain't so much for religion ez it air fer politics" (p. 127). So speaks one Zack Caverly, famed among the locals as "Socrates," and always ready to talk frankly over the crackerbarrel. Fifty pages earlier he had made a similar remark to his friend Elihu Gest, the "Load-Bearer": "After all, I reckon religion en politics air 'bout the same." To which Gest replied: "Sin in politics air ekil to sin in religion—thar ain't no dividin' line" (p. 77).

Elihu Gest is a curious figure, one of the most original creations in all regionalism. Not an ordained preacher, nor apparently a part of the institutionalized church, he is nonetheless universally recognized on the prairie as the community's "Load-Bearer," he who takes up the people's spiritual burdens and carries the extra weight so that there may be community among the settlers. By the time of the camp meeting we have often witnessed his abilities. "A very strange but a very good man," says the boy's mother, with her misgivings about enthusiastic religion, while the boy himself saw that "things which were sealed mysteries to us were finger-posts to him, pointing the way across the prairies, in this direction or that. Is it time to go forth? He would look up at the heavens, sense the state of Nature by the touch of the breeze, sound the humour of the hour with a plumb line of his own, then set out to follow where it led" (p. 50). Elihu Gest had seen Lincoln, too, and knew without presumption the similarity between them:

But somehow it 'peared like Abe Lincoln woud hev such loads ez no

man ever carried since Christ walked in Israel. When I went over fer
te hear him things looked mighty onsartin; 'peared like I hed more'n
I could stand up under; but he handn't spoke more'n ten minutes
afrore I felt like I never hed no loads. I begin te feel ashamed o' bein'
weary en complainin'. When I went te hear him I 'lowed the Lord
might let me carry some loads away, but I soon see Abe Lincoln war
ekil te carry his'n en mine too, en I sot te wonderin' 'bout the
workin's o' Providence (pp. 76-77).

Emulation of Christ *and* Lincoln: a "local Lincoln" prepared to carry the
community's burden of judgment on slavery in the same way Abraham
Lincoln is destined to carry the nation's. In another context the Load-
Bearer might be nothing more than a frontier eccentric, one of the many
comic stereotypes of the ranting country preacher so familiar in western
local-color writing. But in *The Valley of Shadows* he is a serious and compelling character. He is made the dominant force at the camp meeting,
and the reader, no less than the gathered thousands of Illinoisans, must
somehow accept the proposition that Elihu Gest, the Load-Bearer, is to
sit in the place of judgment when the moment of apocalypse arrives.[43]

Grierson's handling of the camp meeting is altogether impressive. He
recognizes the social complexity of the event and in typical genre fashion
presents us with a democratic panorama: throngs of anxious faithful,
isolated groups of sullen Copperheads, drunken rowdies and furtive
whisky vendors, children at play, and, sternly looking out over the mul-
tifarious flock, the elders and preachers. It is a striking regional scene and
a remarkable social phenomenon. The slow progress of the meeting is
given plenty of narrative room, but the climax deserves particular attention. As Elihu Gest had pointed out after the first day's exhortations,
"The people air all right, but they must be tetched" (p. 127). The Load-
Bearer himself spends his time in praying and not preaching, for his position at the camp meeting is irregular. Throughout the second day, and
the third, the spark is likewise wanting, and by Sunday evening the
managers of the meeting are beginning to despair. It is at this point that
Elihu Gest takes over, aided by a providential visitation:

A storm was approaching.... A few minutes more and a squall
descended over the camp and a vivid flash sent a thrill through the
assembly. The crash was followed by a hurricane of shifting light
that swept down closer and closer over the camp. The lightning
seemed to spring from the ground, the air, the woods, the camp
itself.... Just before the hurricane passed away a dazzling bolt struck
the big elm beside the platform. It fell in a blue-white zig-zag. and

to many of the more superstitious it resembled nothing so much as a fiery serpent poured from a vial of wrath overhead, for it split the elm in two (p. 134).

The lightning his cue, the cloven elm his portent, the Load-Bearer ascends the preachers' platform:

> A picture of peculiar fascination was now presented to the wondering and half-dazed people. Arrayed behind the Load-Bearer, in a jagged semi-circle that stretched from one end of the platform to the other, sat all the preachers and exhorters. Witnesses who had once mourned as penitents before the altar now marshalled to make others mourn, as fixed and motionless as statues hewn from syenite; for there was about them something of the mien of Egyptian bas-reliefs seated at the door separating life and death. Some were bearded and grimly entrenched behind a hairy mask; others, in their long, pointed goatees, sharpened the picture; while others again, clean-shaven, and peering straight before them, presented a death-like pallor, at once frail and frightful (p. 134).

This is the equivalent, in frontier evangelical Christian iconography, of the sculptural programs on the tympana of Romanesque cathedrals. Grierson's "picture of peculiar fascination" is a conflation of two familiar visions from Revelation, Christ in majesty and in judgment. Behind the arresting central figure of the Load-Bearer are the "exhorters" arranged in a "jagged semi-circle." The farmer-citizen Elihu Gest has disappeared, for he has assumed the allegorical mantle of the Load-Bearer and will wear it throughout the drama of judgment. The semicircle of preachers is the very semicircle of the twenty-four elders of the Apocalypse, solemnly arrayed behind Christ and ready to see justice dispensed.

From previous chapters, we know that the Load-Bearer has the mystico-ecstatic character of the Savior (for example, as in the west portal of Ste. Madeleine, Vézelay), but this is the time of judgment and he is implacably stern (as at St. Pierre, Moissac): "You are being weighed in the balance! Tophet is yawning for the unregenerate!" (p. 135). Was this to be the time?

> A sensation as if the ground had begun to move and float spread through the multitude; and when, a little later, he cried: "You're hangin' to the hinges of time by a hair!" all doubts vanished. Heads began to droop, bodies swayed from side to side ... people fell to the ground, while stifled groans and lamentations issued from hundreds of throats at once.... The camp resembled a coast strewn

with the dead and dying after a great wreck, and a murmuring tumult alternately rose and fell like that from a moaning wind and a surging sea.

The night of nights had come! It seemed as if hundreds were in the throes of death and would never rise, so that a mingling of pity and dread filled those who had long since professed religion; for the strange union of material and spiritual forces ... the falling away of all worldly props ... rendered ... even the helpers and exhorters speechless (p. 135).

When at long last the welter of emotion subsides and the drama is over, the Load-Bearer becomes Elihu Gest once more, and the people slowly realize it was not the "night of nights" after all, but only a communal catharsis (and almost literally an Aristotelian catharsis: "a mingling of pity and dread filled those who had long since professed religion") through the representation of the *Dies Irae* in backwoods Illinois. Was this a betrayal of the people's expectations? They believed that the Apocalypse was at hand, but were given instead an apocalyptic drama with a little "a." On the other hand a real price was exacted for this "little apocalypse": two deaths during the providential storm show the people how close to the ultimate they were. One of the profligate and profane Wagner boys drowns his body in the creek after drowning his soul in whisky, and, to show the inscrutability of Providence, Alek Jordan, son of the most faithful woman in the community, is struck down by the same bolt of lightning that rent the old elm.

This is Grierson's paradox for Illinois and America. There will be many intermediate apocalypses on the way to the final one. The experience just concluded is neither first nor last. As Elihu Gest puts it, in the final words of the chapter, "Let 'em mourn, let 'em mourn; jedgment ain't far off" (p. 137). The Civil War was imminent, a profounder apocalypse for state and nation, and one that would consume its own Load-Bearer in the holocaust. Yet the people at the camp meeting did not go away unchanged. They were "tetched." They had seen God's judgment on slavery in their own isolated province and were now all the more prepared to accept the abolitionists' prophecy about the coming "terrible swift sword." The landscape "round about Springfield" was also altered. Donati's comet would go back to wherever it came from, the fields would give up their bounty at harvesttime, and from the standpoint of the seasons nothing would be different. But the dark shadow of slavery was about to be lifted: the Underground Railroad would have no more passengers, and in the meantime the dreaded slave-catchers would get no collaboration from the formerly lukewarm, whose hearts had been fired by the events of the camp meeting. The blissful attunement of the boy with nature could finally extend to the larger community. Such was the crucial function of the little apocalypse.

It is appropriate that a recollection of Lincoln concludes the Illinois section of *The Valley of Shadows* (there are a few ensuing chapters that deal with Grierson's experiences in St. Louis and points farther west). His phenomenal rise was the last thing young Grierson saw in Illinois and the thing he carried most vividly with him around the world. At the Alton debate Grierson discerned in Lincoln an unexampled gift for direct and seemingly unrhetorical communication with the people. He saw as well a granitelike moral uprightness and the emanation from him of a kind of American destiny. Lincoln's presence is felt throughout the Illinois chapters of *The Valley of Shadows*, and is felt at times almost as pure spirituality. Oddly enough, however, the chapter devoted exclusively to him is relatively brief and subdued. Grierson speaks of Lincoln's "predestined will," of his "deep mental depression, often bordering on melancholy" (p. 167), but offers few other glimpses into the inner man. In a sense, though, this is appropriate. All along, it has been Lincoln's "natural magic," his "spiritual impulse" that had willed and directed the destiny of Illinois. For Grierson the work is much greater than the man. And Lincoln—no less than the boy and Elihu Gest—is a medium between the ideal and the real.

The Valley of Shadows strongly asserts the importance of place in literature. Though the village on the Illinois prairie remains nameless, though the Grierson farm is impossible to find in the Macoupin County plat book, and though the family passed on into American oblivion after a few years of the agrarian experiment, the remembered place remains vital. The sense of place does not depend on geographical coordinates or archeological detritus. Undoubtedly there was a log house, but what is important, in Grierson's eyes, is the residuum of his Illinois contained in *The Valley of Shadows* itself. The physical landscape is necessary, but the sufficient condition for the romantic sense of place is the dream of Arcadia, the transcendental gateway through nature, and the continuity of past and present. These he embodies in mythopoetic images from the furthest reaches of the West—and not merely the American West. The informing power of the imagination—a boy's intuition, a man's memory, a race's heritage—is the element missing from the Turnerian interpretation of the frontier and the building up of American culture. Were Grierson and his family stripped naked of their inherited culture when they arrived on the frontier? Perhaps there was some element of starting over, but even that activity was shaped by the archetype of the garden, and the rest was more cultural recapitulation than anything else. *The Valley of Shadows* is above all an attempt to ground the sense of place in pastoral and romantic tradition. And in the theme of the little apocalypse Grierson strikingly parallels frontier Protestantism with another period of fundamental Christianity, the Romanesque Middle Ages. After the year 1,000, when the Apocalypse did not come to pass, there was an expansive surge of human energy which resulted in, among other things, some of the greatest apocalyptic art the West has produced. Similarly, after the quasi-apocalyptic drama of the camp meeting comes a time of cultural greatness for Illinois. To be sure, the permanence of the moral lessons of such events is problematic: when the people discover that their apocalypse is a play replayed, there is a thankful catharsis and new energy to be spent. But after a time there is the inevitable backsliding. And Francis Grierson, writing after a time—writing, so he believed, when the last forlorn hope for modern man was to reestablish ties with the romantic and heroic past—would have been aware, as was his contemporary Henry Adams, of the almost unbreachable distance that fifty years can open between a culture's golden age and its later perspective, especially when those fifty years constitute the second half of the nineteenth century.

NOTES—CHAPTER I

1. Christiana Holmes Tillson, *A Woman's Story of Pioneer Illinois* (Chicago: R. R. Donnelley & Sons Co., Lakeside Press, 1919), pp. 21–22. Mrs. Tillson was amused by such enthusiasm but was not the kind of woman to let it pass without qualification: "How would his righteous soul be vexed could he witness the demolition of his Mount Pisgah, through which is made the deep cut called Main Street?" (p. 23).
2. Eliza W. Farnham, *Life in Prairie Land* (New York: Harper & Brothers, 1846), pp. iii–iv. Eliza Farnham's romanticism in *Life in Prairie Land* shows distinct affinities with New England Transcendentalism and deserves serious study in this context. Moreover, her varied career as a writer and a social critic—she was active in prison reform and wrote and lectured for many years on the "woman question"—makes her one of the most important social thinkers ever to discuss emigration to Illinois. See *Notable American Women*, I, 598–600, and the *Dictionary of American Biography*, VI, 282.
3. Compare this to another, less accomplished but equally romantic call to the dispossessed to go west: "To those who awake from the pleasing dream of happiness and security, to the stern reality of a frowning fortune, she would

47

point out asylums of peace and beauty; and invite them to repair, where nature seems waiting to open her stores of rich abundance; to form new hopes, new associations, and new homes" (Catherine Stewart, *New Homes in the West* [1843; reprint ed., Ann Arbor, Mich.: University Microfilms, March of America Facsimile Series no. 68, 1966], p. iv). For both Stewart and Farnham, the West meant the prairies of Illinois.

4. John Stillman Wright, *Letters from the West; or a Caution to Emigrants* (1819; reprint ed., Ann Arbor, Mich.: University Microfilms, March of America Facsimile Series no. 64, 1966), pp. 33–34.

5. There could be an entire book on the aesthetics of the Illinois prairies and their obligatory description in any book of western travel, from Charles Dickens's *American Notes* to the awkward half-literacies or the pseudogeological treatises of some forgotten guides to emigration. Some of the most effective descriptions, however, are by the writers with least literary pretension, including the one by Rebecca Burlend which treats the prairies both from the standpoint of husbandry and landscape. She concludes several pages of description: "Let the reader imagine himself by the side of a rich meadow, or fine grass plain several miles in diameter, decked with myriads of flowers of a most gorgeous and varied description, and he will have before his mind a pretty correct representation of one of these prairies. Nothing can surpass in richness of colour, or beauty of formation many of the flowers which are found in the most liberal profusion on these extensive and untrodden wilds" (Rebecca Burlend, *A True Picture of Emigration: or Fourteen Years in the Interior of North America* [Chicago: R. R. Donnelley & Sons Co., Lakeside Press, 1936], p. 84). Burlend's book belongs with Farnham's *Life in Prairie Land* and Tillson's *A Woman's Story of Pioneer Illinois* as one of the best accounts of the unexampled travails of women pioneers.

6. Arthur C. Boggess, *The Settlement of Illinois, 1778–1830*, Chicago Historical Society Collections, V (Chicago, 1908), pp. 126–27. Gov. Thomas Ford reckoned the population at statehood to be "about forty-five thousand souls," some two thousand of whom were the remnants of the once-flourishing French and Indian groups (*A History of Illinois from Its Commencement as a State in 1818 to 1847*, ed. Milo M. Quaife [Chicago: R. R. Donnelley & Sons Co., Lakeside Press, 1945], I, 32).

7. In 1821 land offices were located at Shawneetown, Kaskaskia, Palestine, Edwardsville, and Vandalia (Boggess, *Settlement of Illinois*, p. 137).

8. James Fenimore Cooper, *The Prairie* (New York: Signet New American Library, 1964), pp. 63–64. On the matter of squatting in early Illiois, Boggess believed it to be "a regular procedure." To protect squatters from total dispossession when the surveying was complete, a preemption act was passed in 1830, entitling squatters who had cultivated their land the previous season to "not more than 160 acres" (*Settlement of Illinois*, p. 139).

9. The story of Birkbeck's important work with the colony at English Prairie, Edwards County, is succinctly told in Theodore C. Pease's *The Frontier State* (Springfield: Illinois Centennial Commission, 1918), pp. 12–17.

10. Morris Birkbeck, *Letters from Illinois* (1818; reprint ed., Ann Arbor, Mich.: University Microfilms, 1968), p. 97.

11. Frederick Jackson Turner, "The Significance of the Frontier in American History," in *An American Primer*, ed. Daniel Boorstin (Chicago: University of Chicago Press, 1966), p. 525.
12. The worship of American nature by people who were otherwise orthodox Christians—a worship complete to the extent of transferring the sacramental structure of the Protestant church right into the wilderness, wood or mountain or prairie—is one of the most remarkable phenomena of American romanticism and has been acutely analyzed by Perry Miller in his essay, "The Romantic Dilemma in American Nationalism and the Concept of Nature" (p. 38 and n. 41 below). For romantic enthusiasts like Eliza Farnham and Catherine Stewart the worship of nature was ecstatic; yet apparently they saw no conflict with the doctrines of conventional Christianity (Stewart's book especially is full of pietistic rhetoric), nor anything heterodox in passages like this: "I wish I could place before you a view I witnessed at sunrise.... Near the termination of a range of hills, a cluster of trees, with massy foliage, stood on the point of a prairie Island; every leaf was baptized with dew; the sun was tinging the topmost branches, while those below, lay in deep shade; flowery arcades sent forth a balmy incense. Through innumerable small islands, the movement of the vessel seemed ever opening some new view of the distant water. It was a perfect picture; and I thought there could be no holier altar for praise and divine adoration!" (Stewart, *New Homes in the West*, p. 83).
13. Birkbeck, *Letters from Illinois*, p. 29.
14. Morris Birkbeck, *Notes on a Journey in America* (1818; reprint ed., Ann Arbor, Mich.: University Microfilms, March of America Facsimile Series, no. 62, 1966), p. 109.
15. Thomas Hubbard, MS Journal, 12 Jan. 1845, Archives, Illinois Wesleyan University Library, Bloomington.
16. Caroline Stansbury Kirkland, *A New Home: Who'll Follow?* (1839).
17. Joseph Kirkland, "Realism and Other Isms," *The Dial*, 16 (1893), 99.
18. This biographical sketch, in the Joseph Kirkland Papers, Newberry Library, Chicago, may have been written by his daughter, Caroline.
19. Letter to Louise Shuler, 15 July 1887, Kirkland Papers.
20. Biographical MS, Kirkland Papers.
21. The actual Grand Prairie extended southward from Lake Michigan to about mid-state (Robert P. Howard, *Illinois: A History of the Prairie State* [Grand Rapids, Mich.: Eerdmans Publishing Co., 1972], p. 5). The Prouder homestead would have been at the prairie's southernmost end.
22. Joseph Kirkland, *Zury: The Meanest Man in Spring County* (1887; reprint ed., Urbana: University of Illinois Press, 1956), p. 6. Subsequent references are contained within the body of the essay.
23. Kirkland may have had in mind the winter of 1830, known as the "winter of the big snow," and remembered for many years to come as the worst "in the annals of early Illinois." The frost came early (September) and the snow stayed late (Howard, *Illinois*, p. 163).
24. Compare Kirkland's rapture with the disappointment of William Oliver, an Englishman who saw the prairies in 1842: "Much has been said of the

flowers 'of every scent and hue' on the prairie, but I must say, that although I saw plenty of weeds, I saw very few flowers of great beauty, and whilst yellow is the prevailing *hue*, the word *scent*, if it mean anything fine, must be taken as a poetical license" (*Eight Months in Illinois* [1843; reprint ed., Ann Arbor, Mich.: University Microfilms, March of America Facsimile Series no. 81, 1966], p. 23).

25. Roderick Nash, *Wilderness and the American Mind*, rev. ed. (New Haven, Conn.: Yale University Paperbound, 1973), p. 2.
26. Nash, *Wilderness and the American Mind*, p. 6.
27. Leo Marx, *The Machine in the Garden* (New York: Oxford University Press, Galaxy Books, 1967), pp. 113–14.
28. Kirkland's *The Story of Chicago* was published posthumously in 1895.
29. But no more ironic than the account of Gov. Thomas Ford, the upright advocate of responsible government, who sat through some of the most blatant demagoguery in the history of the state: "It is a fact well known that one party is governed by the office-holders and the other by the office hunters. Under such circumstances it would be strange indeed if there had been much disposition anywhere to make the future prosperity of the State a consideration paramount.to all others" (*History of Illinois*, II, 107). Ford was governor of Illinois during the years Zury is a legislator and his account (in *History of Illinois*, II, Ch. 2) indicates that Kirkland scarcely exaggerates the situation in Springfield.
30. Kirkland read and admired Thomas Hardy. In the preface to the 1892 edition of the novel, Kirkland admitted that *Zury* was "a palpable imitation of Thomas Hardy's 'Far from the Madding Crowd.'"
31. Among many examples a very readable one, with an improbable title, is *Western Border-Life; or What Fanny Hunter Saw and Heard in Kanzas [sic] and Missouri*, published in 1856.
32. This is the convincing inference of Kenneth J. LaBudde, "A Note on the Text of Joseph Kirkland's *Zury*," *American Literature*, 20 (1949), 454–55.
33. Benjamin Lease, "Realism and Joseph Kirkland's *Zury*," *American Literature*, 23 (1952), 466.
34. Kirkland to Hamlin Garland, 31 May 1887, Kirkland Papers.
35. Turner, "Significance of the Frontier," p. 525.
36. See Francis Grierson, *Modern Mysticism* (1899).
37. From *Modern Mysticism*, quoted in Van Wyck Brooks, *The Confident Years* (New York: E. P. Dutton Co., 1952), p. 268.
38. Francis Grierson, *The Valley of Shadows*, ed. Harold P. Simonson (New Haven, Conn.: College and University Press, 1970), p. 56. Subsequent references are contained within the body of the essay.
39. Bingham painted a series of works as a tribute to western American democracy: *Stump-Speaking* (1854), *The County Election* (1852), and *The Verdict of the People* (1855).
40. The spring of 1858.
41. Perry Miller, "The Romantic Dilemma in American Nationalism and the Concept of Nature," in *Nature's Nation* (Cambridge, Mass.: Harvard University Press, 1967), p. 201.

42. "Even in Arcady there am I," where the "I" is death, according to Erwin Panofsky, "*Et in Arcadia Ego:* Poussin and the Elegiac Tradition," in *Meaning in the Visual Arts* (New York: Doubleday Anchor Books, 1955), pp. 306-7. Compare Grierson's passage with the thoughts of another precocious western boy, Huck Finn: "there was them kind of faint dronings of bugs and flies in the air that makes it seem so lonesome and like everybody's dead and gone; and if a breeze fans along and quivers the leaves, it makes you feel mournful, because you feel like it's spirits whispering—spirits that's been dead ever so many years—and you always think they're talking about *you*. As a general thing it makes a body wish *he* was dead, too, and done with it all" (Ch. XXXII). There is also Whitman's persona of the boy-poet in "Out of the Cradle Endlessly Rocking," to whom the sea whispers the "strong and delicious word," *death*. For all three boys, knowledge of death is necessary if they are to sense what Grierson calls the "thin veil" between phenomenal and noumenal worlds.

43. An interesting "subtextual" confirmation of Elihu Gest's importance in *The Valley of Shadows* is found in Grierson's punning allusion in the name: Elihu, according to one Hebrew rendering, means "He is God." And the most important Old Testament Elihu is a "non-Israelite" (hence an outsider like Grierson's creation) who nonetheless has a prominent voice in the Book of Job (*New Westminster Dictionary of the Bible*, p. 261). Appearing as "one who is perfect in knowledge" (36:4), Elihu rebukes Job in a long and potent speech (32-37) which develops the theme of God's justice, climaxing in an exhortation on His apocalyptic lightning, and ending with these lovely lines about the inscrutability of Providence: "Whether for correction, or for his land, or for love, he causes it to happen"(37:13).

Adding "Gest" to Elihu makes the significance more obvious: God, or God's inspired agent ("one who is perfect in knowledge is with you"), is a guest among the Illinois folk when most they need someone to bear their loads in the troubled times to come.

CHAPTER II

The Town

> These great towns were not built with culture in view, or with
> any thought of the sensitive minds of later generations that
> have risen in them. They were founded, as all towns have been
> founded, since the dawn of history, by aggressive, objective-
> minded men who were seeking an outlet for their primitive
> forces.
>
> —Van Wyck Brooks, *Opinions of Oliver Allston*

Our Towns

It used to be widely believed, at least among intellectuals, that the towns of middle America had no culture worthy of study, nor institutions productive of civilization. Observers, some just passing through, some native sons and daughters, often saw only a wretchedly narrow middle class—a group whose single social goal beyond affluence seemed to be an unhealthy desire to pull everyone down to their level: the nightmare of conformity and group-think. "Middleton" and "Centerville" were sup-posed to have tyrannical, if unwritten, ordinances against eccentricity, and woe to the sensitive mind of heterodox tendencies. Whether or not this was just, it was certainly the predominate literary view of the midwestern town, 1880–1930. Two generations of writers were angry about the "vil-lage virus" and encouraged a wholesale "revolt from the village." Some of the best-known fiction from the period is built around this theme: Mark Twain's "The Man That Corrupted Hadleyburg" (1900), Edgar Watson Howe's *The Story of a Country Town* (1883), Sinclair Lewis's *Main Street* (1920), and Sherwood Anderson's *Winesburg, Ohio* (1919). And, as every Illinois school child knows, the revolt was not confined to fiction: Edgar Lee Masters's *Spoon River Anthology* (1915) used verse to indict the provincial town with stinging effect. In all such writing the social situation of the country town is either treated with scathing sarcasm or forcefully denounced as the cause of a vast human tragedy of arrested development. But all of the writers—functioning as self-conscious social critics—agreed on one point: the town had not fulfilled the implicit utopian promise of the agrarian West. It had betrayed its people, though, they sadly went on to add, the people appeared to have received in the matter just about what they deserved. For the "objective-minded men" who designed and built the midwestern town were complicit in the betrayal.

Looking back to that time now, from the standpoint of half a century or more of continued urbanization (hamlets have become villages, villages towns, and the towns, willy-nilly, are on the way to becoming what urban planners call regional cities), the country town is apt to look quainter to our eyes—still provincial, of course, but provincialism has been made a virtue through nostalgia and is hardly so threatening as had been imagined by the "virus" writers. More often these days the town is recognized as a locus of cultural value and occupies a respected position amid the rectangularly platted farmlands of the Midwest. When the traveler sees from a distance the twin projections of grain elevator and church spire, the evocation is either one of cultural rightness and wholeness or disgust at the obtrusion of another dreary "burg" which will necessitate our slowing down to thirty-five miles per hour. If we allow ourselves to feel positive about the approaching town, it is not from a facile sense of nostalgia for the vestiges of the horse-and-buggy era. Our reaction is far more significant. It is an awareness of the layering of felt life over many successive generations in the same place: these towns are inhabited.

The country towns of downstate Illinois mostly escaped the critical attacks of the antivillage writers. This was not due to any chauvinistic feeling that Illinois's towns were superior, but to the historical accident that no first-rate novelists happened to be concentrating on rural Illinois (they were all busy dramatizing Chicago) when the revolt from the village was a literary fashion. Either fortunately or unfortunately, depending on one's position, Winesburg was in Ohio. True, it might have been moved this way without anyone's noticing a radical difference, for the principal point about the midwestern town was its depressing sameness from state to state and region to region. But in any event the most notorious fictional town in the Midwest remained Ohio's problem. Illinois could, however, boast (or try to disown) the most famous river valley in the Midwest, after Masters put Spoon River on the imaginative map with his volume of wormwood epitaphs, the ironic, embittered words of voices used up by Spoon River and now forever in the grave ("All, all, are sleeping on the hill.").[1] *Spoon River Anthology* is taken for granted as an Illinois cultural monument, a surprising fate for a work that affirms so little in the civilization that has since learned it by heart. Yet whatever else one may wish to say about the region known as Spoon River, in the hands of the poet it became unmistakably a place. As with its slatternly sister town, Winesburg, the inhabitants of that place—definitive grotesques of the American gothic—cannot be forgotten once a reader has been drawn into their strange and disturbing existence. Both places are indelibly marked on the imaginative atlas of the American Midwest.

No such claim can be made for the fiction of the Illinos country town. None of it has the distinction of *Spoon River Anthology*. In the novels and stories concerned with the nineteenth-century Illinois town the fictions center on sentimental or historical romance or on polemics against political and social corruption. The sense of place is inchoate and diluted, and comes through only incidentally in the narratives. But it is the glimmering of place in otherwise egregious local-color fiction that provides the motive for occasional rediscovery.

The Town as Genre—Edward Eggleston's *The Graysons*

By the time Edward Eggleston wrote his *Story of Abraham Lincoln*, as he subtitled *The Graysons* (1887), he had long been established nationally as the Hoosier novelist, and far behind him were such immensely popular Ohio Valley stories as *The Hoosier Schoolmaster* (1871), *The Circuit Rider* (1874), and *Roxy* (1878). Eggleston had been the first and best of the novelists to fashion the local-color materials of antebellum southern Ohio and Indiana, and he would remain preeminent until the rise, after 1900, of the "Gentleman from Indiana," Newton Booth Tarkington. Like Joseph Kirkland, Eggleston had tried several vocations—most notably circuit-riding for the Methodist church in Minnesota—before settling down to a writing career. And like so many of his fellow western writers (Twain, Howells, and Garland in particular) he was self-made and proud of it. He was convinced that the articulation of Ohio Valley culture was a mission too important to be entrusted to college training in the East. A generation before Hamlin Garland sounded the call for a "distinctive utterance" in midwestern literature, Eggleston had attacked invidious eastern attitudes toward his region. In the preface to his first novel, *The*

Hoosier Schoolmaster, he regretted that "the manners, customs, thoughts, and feelings of New England country people filled so large a place in books, while our life, not less interesting, not less romantic ... had no place in literature."[2] Yet in a genial nature such as Eggleston's, this little chip on the shoulder was almost completely unobjectionable.

"I have wished," Eggleston wrote, "to make my stories of value as a contribution to the history of civilization in America,"[3] and throughout his career he maintained that the novel and history were very closely related. In his half-dozen Ohio Valley fictions he treated his local-color materials as respectfully as any historiographer. In him the documentary impulse was so ingrained as to strike some critics as excessive, but he answered them by saying that "the work to be done just now, is to represent the forms and spirit of our own life, and thus free ourselves from habitual imitation of that which is foreign."[4] Today, it is easy to see his point. Eggleston's work constitutes a seminal part of the search not only for a distinctive utterance but for that elusive "usable past" upon which the furtherance of regional culture depended—depended then and now. Long before *The Graysons*, Eggleston had formulated the basic outline of how his local-color art ought to proceed. In the late 1860s he had discovered the work of Hippolyte Taine, the French historian whose *Art in the Netherlands* interested the young writer profoundly. The things Taine was saying about Dutch national art seemed to Eggleston readily applicable to the regional life he had lived as a boy in Vevey, Indiana. He sensed that America was not yet a nation in Taine's organic sense, but rather a composite of regions, each with its own indigenous culture and untapped artistic resources.[5] He soon came to feel, with Taine, that deracination was a fundamental barrier to the realization of great art: "The Dutch painters never produced anything of value in art until they ceased to go to Italy for their subjects and began to paint their own homely Dutch interiors and landscapes and people instead."[6] Hence, when he came to try his first story, *The Hoosier Schoolmaster*, it was already "his fixed conviction that whether in the graphic or in the literary art no man can do his best work unless he chooses for his subject a life which he thoroughly knows."[7] And Eggleston knew the Ohio Valley better than most.

Abraham Lincoln was the greatest individual to come out of the region, and perhaps partly for this reason Eggleston could not escape the literary fascination Lincoln held for hosts of writers before and since. In *The Graysons* he hoped to take advantage of one of the most famous stories of Lincoln in Illinois: the legendary murder trial of Tom Grayson,

Lincoln for the defense, in which he exposes the perfidy of an eyewitness by demonstrating from the almanac that there had been no moon at the time of the murder and that therefore the perjurer could not have seen young Tom Grayson doing the vile deed. This sensation, however, occurs only near the end of the tale. The rest is filled up with Eggleston's characteristic mixture of sentimentalized, impeded young love and delightful genre scenes. By no means is *The Graysons* one of his best novels. Most who read it today do so for the Lincolniana, and though the novel is recognizably Eggleston, the power and authority of *The Circuit Rider* and *Roxy*, a decade before, are notably missing.

Eggleston was always a facile stylist and was used to writing under the pressure of the printer's devil waiting for copy at the door. One senses that by 1887 he could dash off his *Story of Abraham Lincoln* almost effortlessly, for his tried and true approach to local color was becoming formulaic, and he had given up hoping for a masterpiece (he came closest in *Roxy*). But facility can still serve him well, as in the opening "landscape" of *The Graysons*:

> The place of the beginning of this story was a country neighborhood on a shore, if one may call it so, that divided a forest and prairie in Central Illinois. The date was nearly a life-time ago. An orange-colored sun going down behind the thrifty orchard of young apple-trees on John Albaugh's farm, put into shadow the front of a dwelling which had stood in wind and weather long enough to have lost the raw look of newness, and to have its tints so softened that it had become a part of the circumjacent landscape. The phebe-bird, locally known as the pewee, had just finished calling from the top of the large barn, and a belated harvest-fly, or singing locust, as the people call him, was yet filling the warm air with the most summery of all summery notes—notes that seem to be felt as well as heard, pushing one another faster and yet faster through the quivering atmosphere, and then dying away by degrees into languishing, long-drawn, and at last barely audible vibrations.[8]

Eggleston's settings are the narrative equivalent of farmscapes or middle landscapes such as those produced by the painter George Inness early in his career. In *Peace and Plenty* (1865) and *The Lackawanna Valley* (1855) Inness had harmonized nature with the institutions of agrarian and industrial America, contributing in the process to an enduring stylization of the western farmscape. In Eggleston's prose there is the same evocative luminism, a suffusing, nearly tangible late-afternoon light which pervades the scene after the invocation of the required metaphor of the prairie as ocean ("country neighborhood on a shore") and pronounces peace upon the land. The Albaugh farm, we are told, has been in place long enough to have lost its "raw look of newness," and its aspect so "softened" as to have become "a part of the circumjacent landscape." The Illinois farm belongs in nature and no longer shows evidence of having been imposed on the face of the land. Midway through the passage the imagery of light gives way to the sounds of birds and insects, which in turn languish and die away, until all that remains are "barely audible vibrations" in the air and that certain vespertinal quality associated with pastorals.

The analogue with painting is not gratuitous. Eggleston's admiration for seventeenth-century Dutch landscape and genre painting led him to attempt in narrative not only the rendering of common subjects but in the same hearty style of Jan Steen and Theodore Brouwer.[9] It is not too much to say that he thought of narrative in terms of genre scenes—from the first, critics were appalled by his weak plots, and Eggleston was forced to agree[10]—and *The Graysons* is full of them. Over the years he had developed his catalogue of genre subjects until it was basically a matter of which familiar ones to rehearse: should it be harvesttime, farmhouse interiors with the bustle of homemaking, tavern merrymaking, a camp meeting, backwoods electioneering, or any of the whole range of comic stereotypes he had lovingly drawn in his previous books? Any or all of these could contribute to the kind of community he wished to present. In a sense, there are two Illinois towns in *The Graysons*, social poles of the young society which is in the midst of the transition from frontier anarchy to the rule of law. One town is "Broad Run," the locale of the "poor whiteys"; the other is for some reason called "Moscow," and is predictably more respectable: the home of the ascendant Illinois bourgeoisie.

Broad Run is another incarnation of the same low-lived region Eggleston had used in every Ohio Valley novel. It is a magnet for social outcasts, for the arm of the law does not yet reach that far. Though the social historian within Eggleston tried to be disinterested, he could never manage to hide his disdain for the poor-white class and their communities:

> With that instinctive unthriftiness which is the perpetual characteristic of the poor whitey in all his generations, the Broad Run people had chosen the least inviting lands within a hundred miles for their settlement, as though afraid that by acquiring valuable homes they might lose their aptitude for migration; or afraid, perhaps, that fertile prairies might tempt them to toil. . . .
> The Broad Run people entertained a contempt for the law that

may have been derived from ancestors transported for petty felonies. It seemed to them something made in the interest of attorneys and men of property. A person mean enough to "take the law onto" his neighbor was accounted too "trifflin'" to be respectable; good whole-souled men settled their troubles with nature's weapons— fists, teeth, and finger nails (pp. 133–34).

And if such means proved inefficacious, well, there was always lynching. Saved for horse thieves and murderers, this most infamous of frontier expedients was, to the volatile Broad Run folk, perfectly in order for young Tom Grayson, who sat in the Moscow jail accused of murder. Their experience with the law convinced them that Grayson might get off if the issue came to trial, for was there not some damned lawyer (Lincoln!) ready to bemuse an impressionable and naive jury into believing him innocent, and then turn the guilt onto one of their own despised lot? While Eggleston very well knew that there was some justification for the poor-whites' mistrust of the judicial process (after all, they were a minority, and minorities have perennially felt this way, and with reason), his sympathies in the matter are all with the good citizens of Moscow. The invidious comparison between the shiftlessness of Broad Run and the positive industry of Moscow was convenient to Eggleston's literary formula. But it belied his ostensible commitment to social equality and threatened to sour the good feeling of genre: for the Broad Runners, besides being lawless, also manifested most of the animal spirits in the area.

Moscow, Illinois, candidate for future civic greatness, is described in the throes of its postfrontier growing pains:

The village had been planted in what is called an "island," that is, a grove surrounded by prairie on every side. The early settlers in Illinois were afraid to seat themselves far from wood.... the public square was yet a rough piece of woods, with roots and stumps still obtruding where underbrush and trees had been cut out. There was no fence, and there were no hitching-rails. The court-house of that day was a newish frame building, which had the public-grounds all to itself except for the jail, on one corner of the square.... on the side farthest from the jail, stood the village tavern.... In front of the tavern was a native beech-tree, left behind in the general destruction. Under it were some rude benches which afforded a cool and favorite resort to the leisurely villagers. One of the boughs of this tree served its day and generation doubly, for besides contributing to the shadiness of the street-corner, it supported a pendant square sign, which creaked most dolefully whenever there was wind enough to set it swinging in its rusty iron sockets (pp. 172–73).

The sign betokens the "City Hotel," a building which, like most of its fellows in the fledgling town, is completely innocent of paint. Eggleston is reminding us that the town comes after the well-established farms and is to a large extent dependent on them. The crucial question for the town-boosters of Moscow—the "mayor" and "aldermen," but chiefly the land speculators—is whether the town will "take" in the Illinois soil. Or will it be numbered among the hundreds of stillborn villages in the West? Eggleston suggests that Moscow will prosper, because it is peopled by real settlers, men and women with genuine ties to the land, who are beginning to value continuity and staying put with a counterbalancing fervor to the rootlessness prevalent in Broad Run. In the context of *The Graysons* Moscow is destined to grow and Broad Run to disintegrate, its restless Ishmaels cast out once again in search of an ultimate "Pike County" where they might indulge their solitary, sullen insularity. But the foreordained triumph of the Muscovites would, some generations later, make their town, and all like it, more socially homogeneous than their descendants might have wished: in modern, urbanizing America Moscow would find itself on the defensive.

But toward the middle of the nineteenth century, Eggleston insists, a socially inclusive event like a camp meeting could bring Broad Run and Moscow together. Throughout his life, Eggleston maintained a strong personal interest in religion, and his experience on the frontier circuit had led him to many forest retreats and open-air camp meetings—affairs which showed the social complexion of the West more honestly than anything else, even politics. He had used the camp meeting to excellent effect in *The Circuit Rider*. For *The Graysons* he summoned up a picture of western religion at its most convivial:

> In the early days of August there came a time of comparative leisure. The summer harvests were over, and the fields of tall corn had been "laid by" after the last plowing. Then Illinois had a breathing spell.... and in this time of relaxation came the season of Baptist Associations and Methodist Camp-meetings and two-days' Basket Meetings—jolly religious picnics, where you could attend to your soul's salvation and eat "roas'in' ears" with old friends in the thronged recesses of the forests, among a people who were perhaps as gregarious as any the world has ever produced (p. 122).

Picnics in the fine August daylight, but fantastic scenes of soul-saving in the forest night:

> The preaching was vigorous and stirring, and the exhorter, who came after the preacher, told many pathetic stories, which deeply moved a people always eager to be excited. The weird scene no doubt contributed by its spectacular effect to increase the emotion. The bonfires on the platforms illuminated the circle of white tents, which stood out against the wall of blackness in the forest behind; the light mounted a hundred feet and more through the thick branches ... and was reflected from the underside of leaves quivering in the breeze. The boughs and foliage ... had an unreal and unworldly aspect. No imagery of the preacher could make the threatened outer darkness of the lost so weird to the imagination as this scene, in which the company of simple-minded people found themselves in the presence of a savage Nature, and in a sphere of light bounded on every hand by a blackness as of darkness primeval (p. 116).

The night-scene is not only at variance with the sociability of the day, but radically different from the pastoral landscape with which *The Graysons* opened. The almost Manichean division between the golden light of the garden and the "blackness as of darkness primeval" is not something Eggleston develops thematically (as Grierson does), nor is he perhaps aware that he is writing himself into the same universe as Hawthorne and Melville. But it is an interesting coincidence that the camp-meeting scenes in this novel and *The Valley of Shadows* show so many similarities. Each gives us the democratic panorama of all walks of life united by the social phenomenon of the meeting; each has its ne'er-do-wells hanging around the fringes ("In the region of outer blackness ... there were also assemblies of those who were attracted by the excitement, but to whom the religious influences were a centrifugal force. Here jollity and all conceivable deviltry rejoiced also in a meet companionship" [p. 113].); and each presents its religion as fundamental and enthusiastic. So far the parallels are not too surprising, for the genre elements constituted a kind of community property for western artists and writers. More important is the role of Lincoln in both scenes (and both books). As we have seen, Lincoln is a disembodied spiritual force in *The Valley of Shadows*, except for his cameo appearance near the end. In *The Graysons*, of course, he is an active character. Eggleston has the murder happen during the camp meeting, at the height of the exhortations and "in the region of outer blackness" where evil is parasitic on the religion at the center.

Young Tom Grayson, like so many of Eggleston's protagonists, is a man of considerable potential either to be very good or very bad: romantic and impetuous, he has recently gambled and been disgraced, and is in a fair way to succumb to outright evil. To save him, Abraham Lincoln literally uses the fact of darkness at the camp meeting to expunge that evil and set Tom free. And his courtroom act, Eggleston implies, is the cathartic which puts things right with the entire community of Moscow as well. *The Valley of Shadows* shows the spirit of Lincoln at work in the Load-Bearer, but to a similar effect: in both stories he is the redeemer of an Illinois community.[*]

The melodramatic trial of Tom Grayson, Lincoln's surpassing wit in proving a late moonrise on the night of the murder, the acquittal and the resolution of the romances—these are the things that are remembered when Eggleston's *Story of Abraham Lincoln* is remembered at all.[11] This engaging but minor event from Lincoln's Illinois years has passed into the popular imagination to take its place alongside the Douglas debates, the nights of reading by firelight, the railsplitting, and dozens of other folk nuggets which collectively make up the Lincoln myth. Ironically, *The Graysons* is the only story of Eggleston's to have been made into a movie, despite the fact that, except for the Lincoln connection, it is the least likely material of all his work. But the novel needs to be read in the larger context of his entire Ohio Valley literary career, as part of Eggleston's twenty-year determination to study, through fiction, the socialization of the region before the Civil War, building both on his boyhood experiences and an ineradicable notion that the future of American art lay in the humble histories of its locales. With each succeeding novel, reaching a high point with *Roxy* in 1878, he progressed toward a richer conception of his art and a more authoritative statement about his region. The constants in his writing—religion, class-feeling, politics—are in all probability the very features of Ohio Valley life that were indeed paramount. The social insights of the Ohio Valley novels may be said to vindicate Eggleston's view that the novel was a form of social history. A few years after the publication of *The Graysons*, he decided to give up fiction altogether in favor of history. It was an appropriate time to take stock:

> If I were a dispassionate critic, and were set to judge my own novels … I should say that what distinguishes them from other works of fiction is the prominence which they give to social conditions; that the individual characters are here treated to a greater degree than elsewhere as parts of a study of society—as in some sense the logical

results of the environment. Whatever may be the rank assigned to these stories as works of literary art, they will always have a certain value as materials for the student of social history.[12]

Yet, he maintained, the work he would now undertake—he had in mind an historical trilogy on the "transit of civilization" from the old world to the new—"will not differ in essentials from what I have been doing hitherto.... My interest in my work has been that of a student intent upon tracing the forces of life in America to their origins, and showing how men and women lived and thought and felt, under conditions that existed before those of today came into being.... I have been writing history all the time in my novels."[13]

To the end of his days, Eggleston equated purely literary art with smooth plotting, and as a result never fully understood his own graphic powers with landscape and genre and their symbolic authority. To abstract from the fictional context a landscape passage, such as has been done in this discussion of *The Graysons*, is to recognize an important dimension to Eggleston of which he himself was probably not aware. There is much more than social history in his Ohio Valley work. There is locality, in the sense of a distinctive inhabited place that contributes to the overall mythic image of the western farmscape and the country town. It was just this poetic power to synthesize disparate local-color elements into western myth that gave meaning to the kind of social history Eggleston loved. In the end, his inability to plot caused him to fall back on the comforting idea that the novels would serve the future as documentary repositories for new generations of historians and sociologists. In this he undervalued his work. For the synthesis of American culture is finally an imaginative act, and never merely a matter of "palpable realities" in the lives of the western folk.

Booming the Illinois Town—David Ross Locke's *A Paper City* and Mary Hartwell Catherwood's *Spirit of an Illinois Town*

Surely one of the most boisterous phases of western society was that connected with "wildcat towns"—the booming and boosting by land speculators of innumerable prairie towns in which they had vested interests. All such towns were of course certain to become railroad or steamboat junctions, county seats, agricultural centers, or even better! But in reality most of them existed only on paper, and a great many innocents were gulled out of land bounties or life's savings by smooth-tongued town agents who toured their "New Cantons" and "Metropolisvilles" as future—and not too distant future—focal points of American civilization.

In the late 1870s David Ross Locke, creator of the well-known literary comedian "Petroleum Vesuvius Nasby," turned his considerable journalistic talents to novel-writing—avowedly to excoriate political and social venality. He would continue in fiction what he had been doing for some years in his Nasby papers, and, if anything, the novels he began to bring out in those years constituted a more direct attack on the Gilded Age than anything previously issuing from his pen. Unlike most satirists, however, Locke saw scarcely anything to laugh at in the panorama of moral turpitude, and his social indictment extended all the way westward to New Canton, Illinois, the wildcat town of his *A Paper City* (1878).

Nothing is clearer in Locke's fiction than the fact that he is unabashedly using the novel form to inculcate a social lesson in his readers. Hence such artistic amenities as an absence of didacticism on the part of the author, probability of motive in the characters, and causal sequence of events in the plot are outrightly scorned in *A Paper City*. What interest it holds for a contemporary reader derives from its alarming exposé of unprincipled exploitation on the part of western town-planners. If the characterization in the novel is as weak as the greenback dollars issued by New Canton's bank, there is nevertheless a limited fascination in learning just how all this bamboozling was accomplished and how it all came out in the end. The rhetorical power of *A Paper City* resides almost entirely in the author's excoriation of the land company of New Canton, for Locke was determined to show America that land speculation and inflation were often fatally harmful to the commonwealth and the community.

In developing this theme of the dangers of speculation, Locke naturally amplifies on the related theme of the stillborn town—the town with no reason for being and with nothing to hold anyone in it on a permanent basis. New Canton, Illinois, before the land boom was "not a one-horse but a one-mule town."[14] It originally had been "the meanest little town in the state ... which puts New Canton very low in the scale of towns. At its beginning it had a post-office, a Methodist chapel, and a dozen dwellings, set down in the mud and desolation of a wide prairie" (pp. 9–10). The local hosteler, who had never known a paying guest, summed up the situation: "They ginerally come in ridin' in the stage, all so gay; but they ginerally go away on foot. It's curious: people, not only in New Canton, but everywhere, are a-comin' in a-ridin' and a-goin' out on foot" (pp. 9–10). The hosteler is old Petroleum Nasby, of course, commenting this time from the pages of a novel and not from a lecture platform.

New Canton could boast of its "two newspapers, whose editors hated each other like pretty women, and who never agreed upon any thing but the prospects of New Canton" (p. 13). Also productive of civic pride in those boom years of the 1870s were New Canton's "three churches, on very bad terms with each other, but on wonderfully pleasant relations with the world; four lawyers, each of whom spent the most of his time wondering how any man could entrust business with such knaves as the others; three physicians, each of whom in confidence assured everybody else that the others were quacks" (p. 13). And then that one mule.... All this was gratifying in the extreme to the speculators, especially to one Charles Burt, the evil genius behind it all. It was easy for all to see in those delusive years that New Canton was the providential spot for America's and Illinois's future urban glory. And the transformation from one-mule town to metropolis was a thing easily done, what with the magical aegis of paper money, printed at will and with abandon on the subterranean press of the savings bank, a bank which had itself been created *ex nihilo*, without capital and without surety. Such was the buoyancy of spirit in those flush times that the New Canton populace were ready and eager to conjure their future with the hocus-pocus of wild speculation: "New Canton was the moon-ribbed, ill-fed ghost of a city ... begotten by the lying promise of four spectral railroads, on the expectation of an impossible ship-canal. One speculator, with cheek of brass and tongue hung upon swivel; three speculators not so gifted, but equally unscrupulous, with just as little to lose; and one honest but deluded man, adopted the creature, and chattered men into the belief that there was stuff in it for a lusty present and a vigorous future" (p. 13).

The satire in *A Paper City* is laid on plenty thick, overthick in some places. But then America, especially the West, was in its Gilded Age, and could any antidote to the excesses of Grant's administrations be too strong? In his sarcastic onslaught Locke inevitably recalls another and a greater social critic of the day, Mark Twain, who coined the epithet "Gilded Age" in his novel of the same name, written with Charles Dudley Warner and published in 1873. Locke's Charles Burt is clearly overmatched in shenanigans by Twain's Colonel Beriah Sellers, for whom nothing was too big or too difficult. "Spectral railroads" and an "impossible ship-canal" for New Canton? 'Twas nothing beside Sellers's grandiose visions: "The country is getting along very well [he remarked], but our public men are too timid. What we want is more money.... Talk about basing the currency on gold; you might as well base it on pork.

Gold is only one product. Base it on everything! You've got to do something for the West. How am I to move my crops? We must have improvements. Grant's got the idea. We want a canal from the James River to the Mississippi. Government ought to build it."[15] One may wish to laugh at the thought of pork-based money or a transcontinental canal, but the capital irony is that, for once, reality outfantasied fiction: President Ulysses S. Grant proposed just such a canal in his annual message to Congress for 1872![16] Small wonder, then, that as the century stampeded on the satire of men like Twain and Locke became less and less funny, more and more strident and gloomy.

Locke shows that all western bubbles have their bursting, and New Canton can be no exception to an objective law of economics. "You may blow up a bubble, but it will only be a bubble. Soap and water will not harden into marble and granite." David Ross Locke was not a man to let his moral slip by unnoticed, at any rate not one he had been at such pains to illustrate.

> Gone are the milliners, the mantua-makers, the "artists," the "Tattersalls," the "depositories," the "Pharmaceutical establishments," the "palaces," and the other things peculiar to small and ambitious cities; and in their places are a much smaller number of plain dress-makers, photographers, stores, and people, and things of that description—less airy, but doubtless more useful. The "tonsorial parlors" have subsided into barber shops, the "saloons" into groceries. The mighty are fallen indeed (p. 431).

For Locke the decline of New Canton was a judgment the justice of which was almost biblical. The boom had been nothing more than a manipulation of the naive many by the unprincipled few, and a town so founded could not hope to achieve community or permanence, nor would it be a good thing for Illinois for such a town to survive— "mantua-makers" were too far from the vital center of common democratic life in the West. What was needed was a general store and a barber-physician, the one to prescribe homely nostrums and cure-alls, the other to sell them. All else was affectation and mannerism. It was a conclusion also reached by Eggleston in his novel of land-booming, *The Mystery of Metropolisville* (1873): "Taint no land of ideas. It's the ked'ntry of corner lots. Ideas is in the way—don't pay no interest. Haint had time to build a 'sylum for people with ideas yet, in this territory. Ef you must have 'em, why let me recommend Bost'n."[17] And thus the pretentious trappings of high culture were banished from the New

Cantons of Illinois and the Midwest. The towns survived and matured without capital *C* Culture, a fact which before too long instituted itself as a point of provincial pride. But with the twentieth century would come the uneasy question of whether that cultural banishment had been irrevocable. More often than not, the answer appeared to be yes.

Occasionally in fun but mostly in seriousness, David Ross Locke cat-alogued the political sins being perpetrated upon a gullible Midwest by all manner of opportunists. Yet he knew that the problem was not en-tirely one of outsiders taking over a community. He shared Twain's view, expressed in "The Man That Corrupted Hadleyburg," that the natives, in their own greed and narrowness, their venality and insularity, were plain-ly complicit in the exploitation of their regions and towns. His lofty moral purpose made the tone of his local-color considerably darker than that of Eggleston or Joseph Kirkland, who had insisted on positive evo-cations of common western folklife. His satire was as honest as it was tonic, and it is much to be regretted that Locke failed to embody social satire more artistically within the form of the novel. David Locke and his work are lost in obscurity today, with only his satiric persona Nasby sur-facing now and then in histories of the Gilded Age. This is a predictable fate for writers who are too casual in their approach to the problems of composition, for there is a kind of natural selection in the history of art. Only the best survive, and the best are not necessarily the strongest in social criticism. Locke was writing too much for his own time, and that unfortunate fact now makes his books far more curious than compelling.

Mary Catherwood was the only woman writer in the nineteenth cen-tury to sustain a literary career based almost exclusively on the historical and local-color materials of Illinois. She had been born and raised in Ohio, where she was able to get some formal schooling at Granville Female Seminary, but the Hartwells removed to Illinois in the 1850s, and Mary was to be closely identified with the state for the rest of her life. She determined rather early to become a writer, but the deaths of her parents only a few months after the migration to Milford, Illinois, forced her to find some sort of livelihood—resulting, as it did for so many women of the day, in her becoming a schoolmarm and for the time being relegating her writing to the status of an avocation. By 1880, how-ever, she was an established author, with a growing reputation within Illinois and across the land. Though few if any of her titles are remem-bered today, Mary Hartwell Catherwood was, as one of her biographers put it, an "exceptionally ambitious and prolific [author], carrying on several pieces of work at one time." Indefatigable in her literary work, she simply refused to fail, and finally achieved a really "widespread recognition" with the publication in 1889 of the historical novel, *The Romance of Dollard*.[18]

Catherwood's writing dealt with two rather distinct kinds of subject matter. First and foremost were the many stories treating the saga of the French in America, particularly the heroic phase of discovery and settlement of the Illinois country in the seventeenth century: the stirring times of Père Marquette and Joliet. She was fascinated—as Willa Cather would be a generation later—by the French hegemony in the West, by the aristocratic force and steadfastness of the *seigneurs*, and she said as much in a series of historical romances that followed *Dollard*. At first relying on printed sources for her evidence (most notably on the historian Francis Parkman), in later years she traveled frequently to Canada and insisted upon eyewitness accuracy for the details of her fiction. *The Story of Tonty* (1890), *The Lady of Fort St. John* (1891), *Old Kaskaskia* (1893), and *The Little Renault* (1897) are but a few of the titles in which Catherwood chronicled the high romance of the golden age of Franco-American civilization.

But it is Mary Catherwood's local-color fiction that concerns us here. There is almost a conscious sense of contrasting cultures when one turns from, say, *The Little Renault* to *The Spirit of an Illinois Town*, for the latter is as deliberately Anglo-Saxon as the former is French. Perhaps the author felt the contrast as well: the novelettes were published together in the same volume in 1897. In her local-color stories Catherwood attempted to graft her rather ponderous romantic idealism onto the homely materials of frontier Illinois. The result was too often egregious. The rarefied requirements of such romance demanded that, in the case of *The Spirit of an Illinois Town*, a woman who had last seen her lover in Paris should next see him from the window of a train passing through the whistle-stop of Trail City, Illinois. And the cosmic improbability of such a thing was regarded as an artistic virtue by the author. Not a flimsy contrivance, not fictional expediency, but rather something "meant to be." Catherwood was unable to discern the difference between romantic license—something taken by all good writers—and poor structuring. It was a problem that plagued her in nearly every story she wrote.

The Spirit of an Illinois Town is a good case in point. What was the "spirit" of Trail City? Was it civic initiative, manifest destiny, community, or some other form of social boosterism? Not at all: it was one shining star of an idealized girl who, by dying in a tornado, showed the way to reform of a demoralized, deracinated "man with a past." And after her death she wasn't even an abstraction, but a genuine spirit with whom Seth Adams might commune when he was feeling particularly despondent. This sort of nonsense is offensive and intrusive and just about ruins what otherwise might have been a workmanlike tale about the re-Americanization of an expatriate—a man who must learn a new accommodation with his roots and do so within the provincial ambience of Trail City, Illinois.

Yet despite her artistic predilections Catherwood is capable of some fine local-color writing. Trail City is initially described with admirable insight into the process of town-making:

> The prairie was intersected by two railroads, and at their junction, without a single natural advantage, the town sprang up. Neither lake nor stream, neither old woods nor diversity of hills, lured man's enterprise to the spot; nothing but the bald rolling prairie.... Long gaps of vacant lots still showed between buildings. Shopping women had to walk half a mile from the north side to the south side.... On every hand were scattering houses, from mansions having their own gas ... to the rudest shelters of pine, in which owners tabernacled until they could do better; every man's first care being to secure what promised to be the most valuable location he could command.[19]

This might pass for Locke or Kirkland or Eggleston, and, with no hint of what is to follow, the description of Trail City certainly sets up some false expectations in the reader. These expectations are only compounded when Catherwood continues her analysis of Trail City society a few pages later: "The virgin town was still untainted with deep poverty or vice. It had kept itself entirely free ... from that American institution called the saloon, so different from foreign wineshops. We were literally walking through a square mile of Ohio cheer, New England thrift, Kentucky hospitality, New York far-sightedness with capital to back it, and native Illinois grit" (p. 4). *The Spirit of an Illinois Town* is a first-person narrative, and Seth Adams, jaded cosmopolitan returned home, is the narrator. In a nice stroke, Catherwood allows him to set the scene for the novelette through a kind of ironic landscape, similar to those so successfully used by Eggleston, but with the unmistakable difference of being painted by one to whom the prospect is radically new:

> The sun, a plainly defined ball, was melting away in its own radiance, and flattening as it melted, just above the horizon. This

unobstructed setting made weird and long-shadowed effects. I hung back to see it touch ground beyond low buildings. Now it was half gone—now three quarters; now it was a disk of gold—a quivering thread of fire—and now a memory. The wanness of sudden twilight stole eastward. The whole wide land was a map. A freight-train trailed off into glorified northern prairie. The town-herder was bringing cows out of the west, and we could hear farmers' wagons rattling home on the dry autumnal plain. Everybody wore a satisfied grin, because the days of rattlesnake-fighting were over and a long-looked-for millennium had come. Eastward, on a billow of the prairie, a land agent with his swarm of followers could be seen offering lots. Under the clang of locomotive bells and the scattered noises of a skeleton corporation came the suction hint of the note of the bull-goose or thunder-pumper, like a buried village working its pumps (pp. 4–5).

"The whole wide land was a map" is one of the most purely poetic utterances in the Illinois literature of place, the perfect metaphor for the platted prairie lands in their magnificent extent. And the poetry is deftly set off against the narrator's irony ("Everybody wore a satisfied grin, because the days of rattlesnake-fighting were over and a long-looked-for millennium had come") to form a pastoral that is not quite an idyll—tempered just enough by the realization that men—Van Wyck Brooks's objective-minded town-builders—are active in the landscape. This is a memorable passage, and the highlight of the book.

How disintegral the plot turns out to be, when it gets going; how disappointing the change in the characterization of Seth Adams from acute and aloof observer to sentimental adorer of the "shining star" Kate Keene! There is simply no artistic junction between the felt life of the town and the romantic plot. In the beginning Seth Adams is an interesting study, and his struggle to get acclimated to Illinois is honest and moving. On certain bleak winter days he was apt to feel a "sickening distaste" when he arose to meet the "dead level" and "pursuing blackness" of the Illinois plain (p. 33). His depression brings on memories of Europe:

Paris, London, Rome, Florence, called me, with all their art treasures, all their variety of life in which a man might lose himself. Homesickness for things American passed into astonism that man is held to his own place on earth by a cord he cannot break even in a migratory age. His life seems kneaded into that land, and he longs for it when he is away with a reasonless passion that has nothing to do with its adaptability to his physical health or the building of his fortunes. But I was too poor to turn eastward again. The petty treadmill of a country newspaper had me for its automatic motor (pp. 30–31).

This is a sympathetic view of the expatriate American, a person who has no less a sense of place than one closely tied to the prairie, but who can never reconcile that sense with the fact it lay somewhere beyond the limits of his own country. Seth Adams's is the profound "pessimism of a cosmopolite," believably handled by the author. Unfortunately, the cure for that pessimism totally lacks credibility.

For in the moral rehabilitation of Seth Adams, Catherwood relied on the old romantic trick of the transfiguring love of a perfect woman. The history of literature would be considerably depleted without this theme, but in *The Spirit of an Illinois Town* the trick remains a trick and not a masterstroke. Adams merely hears Kate Keene give a dramatic reading at the local Thespian Society program, and the entire bitter history of his life is swept away:

> I worshiped her. The light of God Almighty shone through her.... My trouble was gone.... There was a lambent spirit who had brought the world, the whole world, into this small Illinois town....
>
> I looked around the arctic expanse lost in the vastness of unseen horizon, and loved my town. The semaphore at the railway junction threw crimson lights across the snow, and a hissing of quiescent locomotives came to the ear. Let them plough through darkness on long quests to distant cities. I myself was landed (pp. 60–61).

Perhaps Catherwood sincerely believed that the prairie rose, Kate Keene, had the same romantic power vouchsafed to her as had been the hallmark of idealized women throughout the history of literature (Beatrice, Laura, St. Theresa), but here the momentousness of the effect is surely incommensurate with the cause. For the Illinois girl's characterization owes far more to the American tradition of the blatantly sentimentalized heroine than to the less-crowded one of fully realized women in literature. Catherwood seems hidebound to her romantic formula. And that formula demands death and apotheosis for Kate Keene—hence the contrived but efficacious tornado. Kate's death is convenient in another respect: in death she can be "married" to Seth Adams, a man whom she called father from his resemblance to her late (died-of-drunkenness) parent. When both Seth and Kate lived, holding hands was a dangerous sign of a forbidden physical relationship—was he not, besides being too old for her, so impure from his European adventures as to be utterly unworthy of contact with her snowy flesh? But in death they may respectably be betrothed. Seth may safely be awakened from sleep by the "invisible dear hand of her I love" (p. 105). The sentimental betrayal of legitimate local-color romance is complete.

What becomes of the place, Trail City, Illinois, in all this? Not surprisingly it has been discarded about the middle of the book and is never retrieved. Trail City had indeed been invested with a life of its own, and Catherwood even made a modest attempt, early on, to relate that felt life to the inner consciousness of her narrator, Seth Adams. Had she worked harder at this, the structure of the whole might have been saved from disastrous disunity, for, after all, Adams tells us that Kate's perfect love and power do ultimately make Trail City his place. If we could be made to believe in such a transformation, both the place and the person would take on more significance. Place in literature can never be adequately realized except through the eyes of the person defining it. In *The Spirit of an Illinois Town* it is the carrier between person and place which is missing, and thus the Illinois fictional town with the most potential is left at the end of the novel basically uninhabited.

More than once was this the fate of a story by Mary Hartwell Catherwood. After half a century Dorothy Dondore's judgment of her work holds up: "It must be admitted that she fell into the pitfalls inherent in her favorite *genre* ... she was inclined to refine and sentimentalize her characters too much; and ... her longer novels were marred by structural weaknesses. Nevertheless her books show careful research, a feeling for the untamed background of forest and prairie, and an intelligent sympathy with the past." If she missed out on the mature regional expression of the sense of place which was to come with the twentieth century, she was able to prefigure that later age's almost obsessive interest in the individual's relationship with a community—the western town—he could neither fully love nor ever hope to abandon. This small contribution is enough to cause her to be remembered.

NOTES—CHAPTER II

1. Because these essays are intended as rediscoveries of neglected Illinois literature, *Spoon River Anthology*, as undoubtedly one of the two or three most famous books about the state's culture, is not examined in detail. Its connections with other Illinois literature, past and present, cannot be ignored, however, and *Spoon River* is discussed in the context of contem-

porary Illinois poetry in the concluding section of this work.

2. Edward Eggleston, *The Hoosier Schoolmaster* (New York: Hill and Wang American Century Series, 1957), p. xiii.

3. Edward Eggleston, preface to *The Mystery of Metropolisville* (New York: Orange, Judd and Company, 1873), p. 7.

4. Edward Eggleston, *Mystery of Metropolisville*, p. 7.

5. This was precisely the conclusion that modern folklorists would come to: there was no national folklore in America because there was no ethnic continuity; but there were regions of folklore across the land, one of which was Illinois's "Egypt" in the extreme southern part of the state. A good sampling of "Egyptian" folklore may be found in Richard Dorson's *Buying the Wind: Regional Folklore in America* (Chicago: University of Chicago Press, 1964), Ch. 5.

6. Edward Eggleston, "Books That Have Helped Me," *Forum*, 3 (1887), 584.

7. George Cary Eggleston, *The First of the Hoosiers* (Philadelphia: Drexel and Biddle, 1903), p. 14.

8. Edward Eggleston, *The Graysons: A Story of Abraham Lincoln* (New York: Century Company, 1918), pp. 1–2. Subsequent references are contained within the body of the essay.

9. American genre painters whose work Eggleston might have seen would include William Sydney Mount and George Caleb Bingham among the older, antebellum generation, and Winslow Homer and Eastman Johnson, who were his contemporaries.

10. Earlier in his career Eggleston had written to his wife: "There seems to be general conviction that I cannot plot. I believe that's about right" (George Cary Eggleston, *First of the Hoosiers*, p. 347). Although he worked hard at improving, this maladroitness was something he could never overcome.

11. The actual incidents are narrated in Carl Sandburg's *Abraham Lincoln: The Prairie Years* (New York: Blue Ribbon Books, 1926), pp. 342–45.

12. Edward Eggleston, "Formative Influences," *Forum*, 10 (1890), 286.

13. George Cary Eggleston, *First of the Hoosiers*, p. 105.

14. David Ross Locke, *A Paper City* (Upper Saddle River, N.J.: Gregg Press, 1968), p. 13. Subsequent references made within the body of the essay.

15. Mark Twain and Charles Dudley Warner, *The Gilded Age* (New York: Harpers, 1901), II, 141.

16. See Grant's *Annual Message to Congress*, reprinted in *Appleton's Annual Cyclopedia for 1872*, p. 699.

17. Edward Eggleston, *Mystery of Metropolisville*, p. 21.

18. Dorothy Dondore, writing in the *Dictionary of American Biography*, III, 573–74. I am also considerably indebted to Dondore's *The Prairie and the Making of Middle America; Four Centuries of Description* (Cedar Rapids, Iowa: Torch Press, 1926), a veritable compendium of information on midwestern writing, especially helpful because it discusses writers who are wholly ignored elsewhere.

19. Mary Hartwell Catherwood. *The Spirit of an Illinois Town* (Boston: Houghton, Mifflin, 1897), pp. 1–3. Subsequent references made within the body of the essay.

CHAPTER III

Transition: Going to Chicago

So we are glad to hear that there is a prospect of Mr.
Garland's making his home here in Chicago, where the ramp-
ing prairie winds and the swooping lake breezes contribute to
the development of the humane fancy. Verily there is more
joy in Chicago over the one Garland that repenteth than over
ninety-and-nine Catherwoods that need no repentance.

—Eugene Field, *Sharps and Flats*

The Radical Westerner

"You're the first actual farmer in American fiction—now tell the truth
about it."[1] So wrote Joseph Kirkland to Hamlin Garland in the late summer of 1887, as the latter prepared to return to Boston and his potential
literary career. Kirland was enthusiastic about Garland's prospects, but
even he did not foresee the dramatic impact that the writing of Hamlin
Garland would have on the American popular imagination in coming
years. It took Garland less than a decade (1887–95) to transform American attitudes about agrarian life in the West, as in story after story he
pierced the patina of sentimentality which for generations had surrounded the idea of western American farming. Garland's "Mississippi
Valley" stories, as he called the first collection, *Main-Travelled Roads*
(1891), dramatized for the national conscience a new moral lesson, one
which, according to its author, was long overdue: farming out on his
beloved "Middle Border" region was not all it had been cracked up to be
by the bucolic school of romantic agrarian fiction. And this lesson he
intellectualized with stiff doses of his recent learning in the newfangled
science of sociology and in the dynamic economics of finance capitalism.
Garland was appalled by the entrenched status of a set of agrarian myths
which employed statistics to show that "pianos and Brussels carpets

73

adorned almost every Iowa farmhouse," which stubbornly insisted that "tilling the prairie soil was 'the noblest vocation in the world,' " and which accused this "first actual farmer" of befouling his own nest by attacking the western utopia.[2] Years after the storm over *Main-Travelled Roads* had passed, Garland recalled his own radical's contempt for those who refused to see the cruel western landscape in the clear light of objective economics: "True, corn was only eleven cents per bushel at that time, and the number of alien farm-renters was increasing. True, all the bright boys and girls were leaving the farm, following the example of my critics, but these I was told were all signs of prosperity and not of decay. The American farmer was getting rich, and moving to town, only the renters and the hired man were uneasy and clamorous."[3]

Garland, almost uniquely among the writers of his day, was able to see the agrarian dilemma partly in terms of social class conflict, partly as the result of the inexorable march of finance capitalism, and he did so without sacrificing the finer points of his art to the cause of polemics. Where on earth did he get such ideas, this untutored son of the Wisconsin coulees[4] and the Iowa corn rows? And why did the betrayal of the agrarian dream cause him to rebel so angrily and indeed precipitate him into a writing career he might otherwise have missed?

The answer lies in the fact that Hamlin Garland sincerely loved the land and at times was full to bursting with western sentiment. Yet his intellect was thoroughly radicalized by his studies and experiences in the East. These two conditions formed a kind of critical mass within him, a fierce amalgam of West and East that had to find expression. The result was something new in American literature: the drama of agrarian defeat and dystopia.

Part of the credit for Garland's early direction goes to William Dean Howells. When, in the mid-1880s, Garland came East with, as he thought, a proxy in his pocket to speak for the glorious but oppressed West, he was doing the same thing that the older Ohioan, Howells, had done twenty years before. In the cause of western American realism Howells was indefatigable and almost universally sympathetic: and he befriended young Garland as he would befriend the dozens of other aspirants who sought him out over the years. In Boston Garland found Howells approaching the pinnacle of his career, a career devoted to advancing the story of the "common mass of men" in American literature. The two writers, one proven, one untried, were an important generation apart and represented in 1887 the rural and urban cultural poles of American life, though both had in common their western origins and their self-made status. Yet scenically removed as they were from one another, Garland and Howells shared an ideology of literature. Both men understood realism to mean about the same thing: just as, according to Howells, a writer could not ignore such events as the "civil murder," as he termed it, of the Chicago anarchists,[5] overflowing with social ramifications, so, Garland felt, the realist could not turn his back on the "land monopoly" that was crushing the western farmer ruthlessly "under the lion's paw." For were these not, after all, related phenomena, ultimately effects of the same baleful cause, finance capitalism? Fortunately, however, both writers took their fiction beyond politics and economics. Unabashedly democratic, they tied politics to the national character and tried to embody the acting out of this ethos in their stories. The realist's artistic imperative, they agreed, was not simply to get the facts of the American experience straight, but to unfold through dramatization the complex implications of those facts. Howells's friendship for Garland had just enough of the paternal in it to assure the younger man's learning something from the older. And Garland could have learned nothing more important than Howells's honest but penetrating view of the American character: "We are all, or nearly all, struggling to be distinguished from the mass, and to be set apart in the select circles and upper classes like the fine people we have read about. We are really a mixture of the plebeian ingredients of the whole world; but that is not bad; our vulgarity consists in trying to ignore 'the worth of the vulgar,' in believing that the superfine is better."[6] William Dean Howells got an empirical verification of his perception as every day he walked the teeming streets of Boston and New York, and the point of "the worth of the vulgar" would not be lost on Hamlin Garland when, some years later, he attempted to write an urban novel of his own.

But Garland also got good advice on his writing and on the salient features of late nineteenth-century American life from another of his literary friends, Joseph Kirkland. By the accident of a review of an unknown writer's first novel, Garland established a correspondence with Kirkland which soon led to a warm companionship between them. When the Chicagoan heard of Garland's generous review of *Zury* in the Boston *Evening Transcript*, he immediately wrote him, expressing amazement that "an Eastern man" could understand western rural life so well and so sympathetically.[7] Garland, of course, was only temporarily in exile in the East, and took up Kirkland's invitation to call on him the next time he was in Chicago. They were friends from the first meeting. Kirkland, in a letter to his vacationing family, humorously recalled Hamlin Garland's first visit. He came bristling with untried notions about a new "democratic literature" for America: "Enthusiast—country boy—farmer's son—largely self-educated—wants to reform the literature of our country! Reconstruct it on realistic basis. Hates Lowell, Holmes, and all the other fossil representatives of classicism. Loves Walt Whitman and Howells and Howe . . . and *me*. Has a great work on hand 'Literary Democracy' apotheosis of common things and common people."[8]

Along with many other plans of his sanguine youth, Garland's "Literary Democracy" somehow did not get realized, though plenty of earnest pieces did soon begin to flow from his active pen. Perhaps Joseph Kirkland took so readily to the young Garland because, in a sense, he was Kirkland himself brought up to date. Through the younger man's eyes Kirkland could see his Illinois in the broad daylight of the here and now, rather than through the smoky glass of retrospection, for he saw in his "actual farmer" the first writer in the entire West to insist, and insist stridently, upon strict contemporaneity in his fiction. The custodianship of the past was all very well, but Garland's radicalism—like all radicalism—demanded the truth about the present in the interests of a better future. Kirkland rightly understood that he had begun too late to catch up to the present condition of western agrarian life, but he delighted to revel vicariously in a radicalism he could never himself either live or write. Kirkland continued to admire and support his young protégé until his death in 1894.

The intellectual expression of Hamlin Garland's agrarian radicalism is contained in *Crumbling Idols* (1894). Though it was published after his removal to Chicago, the essays contained in *Crumbling Idols* were mostly the fruit of long sessions of intense thought at the Boston Public Library, where over a course of three years or so Garland educated himself and prepared to return to the West. Amid the stacks of books on his reading table—Darwin, Herbert Spencer, Henrik Ibsen, Hippolyte Taine were his representative authors—one can imagine Garland pausing over some particularly striking passage to cast his imagination back to the coulees and the cornfields, wondering what the Middle Border needed in the way of a culture. What would its distinctive utterance be? Out of such long spells of thinking and reading and brooding came the essays of *Crumbling Idols*.

The work constituted an intellectual manifesto, a clarion call to full cultural independence for the West. Garland chose to speak to the generation of writers who would follow in what he hoped would be his pioneering footsteps, and though this seems amusing and presumptuous in a writer still as green in literary matters as Garland was at the time, he confidently announced to the world both principle and procedure for the new literature, and in the process unmistakably echoed one of the cardinal ideas of Edward Eggleston: "Art, I must insist, is an individual thing.—the question of one man facing certain facts and telling his individual relations to them. His first care must be to present his own concept. That is, I believe, the essence of veritism: 'Write of those things of which you know most, and for which you care most. By so doing you will be true to yourself, true to your locality, and true to your time.'"[9] The idea of the personal in art—of the artist's having "his own concept"—is by now one of the familiar antitraditional dogmas of modern art. Its influence has led to a modicum of good writing and painting but has also helped give rise to an immense body of mediocre art or worse; for the great chain of being linking past and present in art, once severed, leaves the lesser artist with little or nothing to say, no matter what the refinement of his technical faculties. But the second idea in this passage, the idea of roots in art, directly connects Garland (however inconsistently) with an American tradition which is itself grounded in European culture. With typical lack of system the outspoken young writer would deny his past and have it too. Hamlin Garland sincerely believed that there might be a literature of locales and regions that nonetheless, in its individuality, owed nothing to past evocations of the same locales or to the general idea of the sense of place in literature.

The iconoclastic energy of *Crumbling Idols* is nowhere more strongly felt than in Garland's attack on the established order of education in America. "It can almost be stated as a rule without exception that in our colleges there is no chair of English literature which is not dominated by conservative criticism, and where sneering allusion to modern writers is not daily made."[10] It was an attitude he found particularly galling in the West, where chauvinistic professors were apt to tell their students that no American literature written west of Cambridge was fit to read, let alone study. Only the Boston Brahmins and New England "Good Grey Poets" were taught, and these venerables were presented to western schoolchildren with a reverence Garland thought precisely owing to their derivation from English models. Meanwhile, American originals like Walt Whitman—whom he had also discovered in the Reading Room of the Boston Public—were being ignored or even proscribed.[11] This was not merely unwestern, he declared, but un-American as well. Garland shared the western American's almost mystical faith in public education as the shoring force of democracy—"The means of education shall forever be encouraged"[12]—but what was taught had better be appropriate to the felt life of the region. A good education was certainly necessary for the coming-of-age of his Middle Border, but in 1894 Garland was convinced it was nowhere to be found.

In the later essays of *Crumbling Idols*, some of which were written in Chicago, Garland turns his attention to the elusive Great American Novel, addressing in hopeful fashion the perennial questions of when, where, and by whom it would eventually be written. Not surprisingly he places his bets on the regionalists of America. "In the north the novel will continue local for some time to come. It will delineate the intimate life and speech of every section of our enormous and widely scattered republic; it will catch and fix in charcoal the changing, assimilating race, delineating the pathos and humor and the infinite drama of their swift adjustment to new conditions."[13] His new life in Chicago was beginning to suggest a fact that would be a revelation to Garland: its ghettos and neighborhoods and business districts were little regions, much like the Wisconsin coulees, and equally amenable to treatment in a literature of place. He went on to suggest that the great urban American novel could never be written by a "tourist and outsider," for this was a job for someone wholly immersed in the rhythms of city life. Ironically, he was perhaps suggesting that such a novel could not be written by Hamlin Garland.

Crumbling Idols concludes with a soaring prophecy of things to come in American art. It is the prosaic equivalent to Whitman's poetic optimism concerning the fulfillment of democracy in the West. Disturbed as he undeniably was about the life of the small farmer, Garland could not suppress his utopian vision for the new age in western art:

> There is coming in this land the mightiest assertion in art of the rights of man and the glory of the physical universe ever made in the world. It will be done, not by one man, but by many men and women. It will be born, not of imitation, nor of fear of masters, nor will it come from homes of great wealth. It will come from the average American home, in the city as well as in the country. It will deal with all kinds and conditions. It will be born of the mingling seas of men in the vast interior of America, because there the problem of the perpetuity of our democracy, the question of the liberty as well as the nationality of our art, will be fought out. This literature will be too great to submit to the domination of any literary centre or literary master. With cities of half a million inhabitants scattered from Pittsburg to Seattle, New York and Chicago will alike be made humble.[14]

Maybe "Literary Democracy" was written after all! Fine words and ringing phrases here, but it is difficult today to discern just to whom Garland
was speaking. The rhetoric seems excessive and overoptimistic. Such a
grandiose program, one of battles "fought out" "in the vast interior of
America," would be seen after the turn of the century as both naive and
bloated. For the simple fact is that Hamlin Garland ended rather than
founded a lasting literary tradition—a strange fate for a writer who
thought he was leading a revolution. To confirm the almost total eclipse
of Garland's regionalism one need only consider the scornful manner in
which Ernest Hemingway, though a scion of the region Garland was
talking about, chose to refer to the Midwest in his literature. And
Hemingway's artistic Midwest has prevailed in the twentieth century.
No homegrown democratic literature of distinction was immediately
forthcoming in the way Garland expected, and he lived long enough to
see his mistake. Yet he never ceased believing that American literature
would have been better off walking his main-traveled road instead of the
myriad others it chose. In 1894 all was colored by his radical enthusiasm
and by the imagined brotherhood his politics would create. And Hamlin
Garland had one more major contribution to make toward the realization
of his expansive social and literary notions. In those first months of
residence in Chicago he put polemics aside and began working very hard
on a new novel which he felt would be perfectly programmatic of both
"veritism" and "democratic literature." For the first time in his life he
would attempt to speak broadly, synthetically about both country and
city and would tell the world the truth about the modern-age cultural
dependence between them. With more than forty years of writing ahead
of him, Garland could not have foreseen that the work in question would
turn out to be at once an artistic culmination and high-water mark and
his last major fiction to be set on the Middle Border.

Rose of Dutcher's Coolly[15]

Hamlin Garland had arrived in Chicago at the height of the stunning
World's Columbian Exposition and was soon as involved in its magic as
the rest of the population. He engaged to give a paper for the Congress of
Literature at the fair, as Chicagoans were calling the exposition, and his
"Local Color in Fiction" was a renewal of the western polemics he had
been conducting at a distance from Boston. The speech was, predictably,
a direct attack on the bucolic school of local fiction, as represented by

Mary Hartwell Catherwood. Garland at that time was finding all such literature jejune and even morally offensive. But Mrs. Catherwood had already had her say in an earlier essay, and Garland could not deny that her position was well bolstered by the cold empiricism of sales, while he, on the other hand, was a radical subsisting on ideology rather than a steady income. He discovered that being a writer was an empty-pursed distinction if one were not also an "author." He very much needed to make his accommodation with the reading public, but how might this be done without the ethical paralysis of compromised principles? Eugene Field's bantering predictions concerning Garland's "repentance," voiced in his witty and urbane column in the Chicago *Daily News*, were in fact borne out, and the "domestication" of Hamlin Garland, as Larzer Ziff has called it, was soon well under way.[16] The earnest spokesman for the New West was soon being vigorously lionized by the very social classes he was busily and noisily indicting in *Crumbling Idols*. For the fair year in Chicago was also a year of inveterate socializing among the quality, who showed remarkable industry and capacity in absorbing the manifold cultural attractions of a worldwide exposition. Garland was one of these curiosities. And the young man was anything but sophisticated, apt to stumble into what seem to us amusing and petty social perplexities, but which were to the gravely self-serious artist matters of moment. At one point he agonized for two weeks over the problem of proper dress for a literary reception at Mrs. Potter Palmer's, and even his good friend and fellow novelist Henry Blake Fuller could not resist joking about the country boy's bewilderment over social punctilio (in the short story, "The Downfall of Abner Joyce," *Under the Skylights*, 1901). But from the humorous accounts of Garland's social initiation two important facts emerge: his career was undergoing profound change, away from the earlier agrarian radicalism, and the young writer was trying hard to embody some positive view of the individual in society in his art.

The result was *Rose of Dutcher's Coolly*, easily his finest long fiction and the last of his Middle Border tales, since after 1895 he would abandon the region in favor of a new far western and Rocky Mountain setting. Garland tried to put into the novel all that he had learned about the trials of agrarian life in the Coolly region of Wisconsin, but this was to be balanced by a newer knowledge of the pulsating, burgeoning life of urban Chicago. Moreover, the settings were to be largely subordinated to the story: the emerging new woman of turn-of-the-century America. *Rose of Dutcher's Coolly* was intended as a probing character study of a woman in two different environments, the rural and the urban, and, though not strictly a problem novel, it would address the question of whether the twain might somehow meet; that is, whether the city-country axis might produce a more fully human person than either alone. *Rose* the novel and Rose the heroine both give emphatic affirmation of the continuity between country and city in the Midwest. The novel today meets or surpasses Garland's expectations, and it shows the author at his most positive about American society: a rural childhood and adolescence, an urban finishing, a whole person.

The precocious personality of Garland's Rose dominates the novel from the outset. *Rose of Dutcher's Coolly* begins with the heroine's girlhood on the Dutcher farm near Tyre, Wisconsin: the formative influences of the earth; the "pagan-free" growth of body and spirit under the bright coulee sun. "When the days were hot they [boys] could go down there in the cool, nice creek, strip and have a good time, but girls must primp around and try to keep nice and clean. She looked longingly at the naked little savages running about and splashing in the water. There was something so fine and joyous in it, her childish heart rebelled at sex-distinction as she walked away. She, too, loved the feel of the water and the caress of the wind."[17] She is depicted as precocious in every way. Rose is bright, strong, and healthy. She has fancy; she feels. Very early on in the novel we can see that hers is to be a major life, and that Rose will live through articulating the instincts of the natural woman: "Sometimes when alone she slipped off her clothes and ran amid the tall corn-stalks like a wild thing. Her slim brown body slipped among the leaves like a weasel in the grass. Some secret, strange delight, drawn from ancestral sources, bubbled over from her pounding heart, and she ran until wearied and sore with the rasping corn leaves" (p. 19).

This passage plainly deals with the awakening of female sexuality in a child and is one of the franker attempts at revealing the psychic truth about one of the forbidden subjects in Victorian America. Garland's characterization of an adolescent Rose anticipates by four years the more famous treatment of the same subject by Kate Chopin in *The Awakening* (1899).[18] But the essential difference between the two novels is that Garland kept Rose almost mystically free from actual sexual involvement after adolescence—no sex before or outside of marriage—while Chopin courageoulsy sent her Edna Pontellier on a sensuous journey of exploration of her adult body: a journey which, though ultimately unfulfilling, did not preclude adultery. Both writers, however, agreed on the primacy of childhood sexuality as a major structuring influence on the adult personality. Their respective treatments of the subject were a striking prefigurement of what in the twentieth century would become a kind of modern literary commonplace, the use and abuse of Freudian psychology.

Because of the glorious and all but illimitable freedom of farm life, because she is motherless, there is nothing that can be hidden from Rose Dutcher's quick apprehension. She takes in everything, and it is only from some innate moral sense—part of Garland's mystique for Rose—or from the occasional negative gestures of her taciturn but adoring father that she can begin to discern the conventional social distinction between good and evil. For in Rose, as in Huck Finn, intuition is the moral arbiter—intuition in mysterious communication with nature—and Garland stoutly sides with Mark Twain in deeming it more reliable than anything society's institutions can provide: "Before her eyes from the time of her toddling youth had proceeded the drama of animal life. She had seen it all; courtship, birth, death. Nothing escaped her keen, searching, inquisitive eyes. She asked her father about these dramatic and furious episodes of the barnyard, but he put her off, and she finally ceased to ask about them. She began to perceive that they were considered of that obscure and unmentionable world of sin, with which men and men alone had the proper right to deal." And if the "apparently shameful fact of sex faced her everywhere, yet through it all she lived a glad, free, wholesome life. Her blood was sweet and clean and kept off contagion. Her brown skin flushed with its unhindered current. She dipped into this obscure questionable world only momentarily" (pp. 22–23). The land was fashioning a beautiful and noble woman out of the best raw materials. Where would such youthful passions as Rose's be more likely given free rein than in a situation so necessarily tied to nature? And where would such freedom be less likely to corrupt? But where also would it be given—by those who mistrusted feeling and nature—some darkly grotesque overtones, if not in the lonely and silent Coolly region, in backroad areas where the church itself, so bleakly empty of passion, a kind of Protestantism gone to seed, suggested some counterprinciple of antilife or evil? Garland, however, was having none of original sin for the woman on the Coolly or for the Coolly itself. And he makes it plain that neither John Dutcher nor his perfect daughter will have anything to do with the local Protestant church, though hinting all the while that their apostasy is more than a little mortifying to the community. Rose receives the grace of her vast spirituality from the land and the land alone, while the father takes a measure of solace from watching the beauty of his daily growing Rose.

With the land as moral tutor Rose hardly needed the institution of the church, even in the matter of developing sexuality. She kept her sometimes profound awareness to herself and privately wondered at its epiphanic presence within: "She felt a terrible hunger, a desire to take his head in her arms and kiss it. Her muscles ached and quivered with something she could not fathom. As she resisted she drew calm, but mysteriously sad, as if something were passing from her forever. The leaves whispered a message to her, and the stream repeated an occult note of joy, which was mixed with sorrow" (pp. 31–32). Her resistance to adolescent passion leads to the adult perception of melancholy beauty, as once again the land reinforces the rightness of her moral intuition. The aching denial of the youthful sexual impulse becomes the prelude to the grand passion of the woman, a passion which in Rose's case is most certainly destined to be.

Garland's treatment of Rose's sexuality as a girl is as frank as it is positive, and remarkably honest for the literature of the day. Hence it is with pleasure that a contemporary reader notes the fact that an Illinois writer is breaking new artistic ground in American literature with the supremely important subject of American womanhood—and doing so before the turn of the century. Inevitably, Garland's forthrightness about sexuality in *Rose of Dutcher's Coolly* was too much for many among his audience and his critics, who rushed to call the novel "indecent" and "immoral." A similar but more severe fate was accorded Chopin's *The Awakening* a few years later. No matter how magnificently written, no matter how splendidly moving the tragedy, contemporary readers were not ready to accept the representation of sexual discovery in women. With the often priggish literary audience of late nineteenth-century America, the merest hint of such a thing was enough to call down damnation on a novel, for even such tepid works as Eggleston's *Roxy* and Kirkland's *Zury* were so attacked, while more daring fictions—notably Theodore Dreiser's *Sister Carrie* (1900) and Robert Herrick's *Together* (1908)—struggled to find any audience at all outside the small circle of liberal literati. It was a cultural stasis which would only be broken by the cosmopolitan shocks of World War I and the "lost generation" that followed.

Part of the "occult" message whispered to Rose by the land is a first calling to a vocation: she would be a writer. And her desire is confirmed and intensified by an idealized infatuation for a touring circus performer, William de Lisle, whose gaudy troupe visits Tyre and turns the romantic head of the Coolly girl. She is deeply affected by this "Knight, like Ivanhoe," who offers her an almost blinding glimpse of the world beyond the Coolly: "Rose shuddered with a new emotion as they swept past. She had never looked into eyes like those.... They rode straight out of the wonder and mystery of the morning to her. They came from the unknown spaces of song and story beyond the hills" (p. 48). Here was romance which seemed to show Rose the way. To her the spectacle was not the tawdry retinue of an itinerant circus, with its quite dubious human and animal populations, but rather a revelation and a gift from the greater world. With the fervor of an adolescent St. Theresa Rose consecrates her life to William de Lisle, whom she will forevermore carry around in her imagination like a guiding icon. Her ideal will help her become a writer: "She would write books like *Ivanhoe*" (p. 61). This sort of romantic idealism, as we have seen in the writing of Mary Catherwood, has its perilous pitfalls, both personal and literary. When Mark Twain quipped that Sir Walter Scott had been the principal cause of the Civil War, he had in mind just this sort of romanticism, and indeed Garland had nothing good to say for it in the writing of others. Yet what saves Rose's idealism from being banal is its individuality, for with her it is a personal and a private matter, not codified into foolish social dogma nor psychically intensified into the obsession that has become the modern romantic temperament in literature.[19] In Rose we feel that the idealization of William de Lisle will be productive of continuity between the later present of adulthood and the remembered past of childhood. At any rate this is what Garland surely intends, and it is difficult to oppose his design. His artistry in these pages makes it very hard to say, as we would of so many romantics, "What claptrap, what a silly girl." Naive as it is, Rose's romanticism is dramatically necessary: and it is the natural imaginative leap into the world from childhood's protective nurture on the land.

Rose, however, writes no *Ivanhoes*. Years afterward, when she begins to write in earnest, it is not from the hackneyed old romantic formulas but with a new sense of the importance of Coolly themes in a Coolly setting. That her own backyard is a proper literary province is a realization which comes only after she has twice left the homeplace behind: first for college at Madison, then for the wider horizons of Chicago. The resonant paradox of leaving one's homeplace in order to realize its intrinsic worth is one that informs *Rose of Dutcher's Coolly* and helps structure the heroine's complex inner development. Rose "expatriates" herself not so much to learn what to write about, but to gain an inkling of how legitimately to embody the emotions of self and place in her poetry. This, recognizably, had been Hamlin Garland's own pilgrimage to Boston. But a girl who would be a woman and independent constitutes a much more significant emancipation. There had been nothing the least irregular in Garland's leaving the farm. His brothers could take up the slack, or so he thought. But a woman's going to the city, and going with professional notions of a career as part of her baggage, was something of an eyebrow-raiser before the turn of the century. Rose escapes the lifelong drudgery (the very drudgery which had first bent and then broken Garland's mother and sister)[20] of a too-early marriage to the plodding farmer, Carl, who had been her first boyfriend. Garland knew from experience that such a leaving was humanly needful, and the alternative of staying put and marrying was, for one of Rose's potential, too appalling to contemplate, no matter what might be the future of the Dutcher homestead or even the agrarian community of southern Wisconsin. It was tacit admission that the myth of the yeoman farmer and his wife and his family living a fulfilling life in the garden of the world no longer sufficed. For Hamlin Garland the farm could never again symbolize the best or the definitive in American culture.

John Dutcher saw this fact more clearly than his daughter: "It was the bitterest moment of his life, since his wife's death. His eyes were opened to his fate; he saw what he had done; he had educated his daughter out of his world. Never again would she be content in the coolly beside him. He saw how foolish he had been all these years, to suppose he could educate and keep her." But the fast aging farmer—he would be the last of the Dutchers on the Coolly—"reached to a divination of the fatality of it all. It had to be, for it was a part of it all. It had to be, for it was a part of progress" (pp. 177–78). John Dutcher saw the fatality in his and Rose's condition and saw as well that it was the fatality of the West. But he could not affirm his fate. Rose's departure from the Coolly for Chicago simply must be seen on its symbolic level to be fully understood. The agrarian myth out West was by the 1890s running as dry as the coulees in summer. The blissful promise of a perfectly pastoral human community had been obviated by the industrial revolution and its concomitant economics. From that point on in American life the land might still nurture its children but must expect to lose them sooner or later to the greater world. And for uncounted thousands that world was Chicago.

Initially Rose headed for Chicago because, as she supposed, "the lake was there; art was there, and music and drama—and love! Always under each emotion, always behind every success was the understanding that love was to be the woman's reward and recompense" (pp. 180–81). Still swimming in romanticism: and were she less impressive a creation we would be dealing with merely one more in that endless procession of innocent country girls toward the manifold dangers of the wicked Big City. But rather than sentimentalizing her cultural shock, Garland describes it with naturalistic honesty: "The cars thickened, the sun grew hot and lay in squares of blinding light across her carpet. That curious pungent smell came in with the wind. Newsboys cried their morning papers. Children fought and played in the street. Distant whistles began to sound, and her first morning in Chicago came to Rose, hot, brazen, unnatural, and found her blinded, bruised, discouraged, abased, home-sick" (p. 192). As all newcomers who would presume to know the city, Rose must become acclimated to the exasperating chaos of urban life. She will be "bridged" trying to get to the Loop, will be daily besooted, face and clothes, and will in short experience the alphas and omegas of Chicago existence. "So it was—the wonderful and the terrifying appealed to her mind first. In all the city she saw the huge and the fierce. She perceived only contrasts. She saw the ragged newsboys and the towering policeman. She saw the rag-pickers, the street vermin, with a shudder of pity and horror, and she saw also the gorgeous show windows of the great stores" (p. 205). The immense drama of urban polarities is a new but equally sensuous kind of grist for the country girl's imaginative mill, and, were it ever so overwhelming to most, Rose would take the city whole.

But the city is not the country, and Rose is vouchsafed a guide for her initiation into Chicago's mysteries. Throughout the novel Garland has conveniently provided Rose with role-models and benevolent protec-tresses (for example, the "famous woman lawyer" who saves her from the "mashing" of a train conductor during Rose's first journey from the Coolly to college in Madison), and never has the impressionable farm girl needed help more desperately than in her first unsettling days in Chicago. To the rescue Dr. Isabel Herrick: significantly the third professional woman of distinction to bolster Rose and adopt her as a protégé. First professors, then lawyers, and now doctors—women all of them—who provide exciting examples of independent career persons for the high-aspiring Rose. Dr. Herrick is the novel's most brilliant "emancipated woman," one who has challenged male prejudice in its most formidable bastion, the medical profession. Yet at first the woman doctor misjudges Rose. On the occasion of Rose's appearance at her office, letter of intro-dution in hand, the newcomer blurts out her inchoate desire to be a writer, and the older woman's seasoned response is a resounding "Write! My dear girl, every addlepate wants to write" (p. 209). To this undeni-ably just observation, however, Rose replies with spirit and a head held high, and the doctor soon perceives her real mettle and depth, and deter-mines to introduce her into Chicago's "better" society—much as Garland himself had so recently been inducted into the city's social circles.

Rose is properly humble at the prospect, but in no way daunted. Her native pluck is nowhere better shown than in the delightful scene of her first dinner in "good company": she contributes for the parlor entertainment of that select group an exhibition of down-home country whistling! As it turns out, the gathered sophisticates need a bit of a return to the roots, and Rose's whistled country-dances are an absurd success in the fashionable North Side home of Dr. Herrick. After the whistling comes the poetry, and the verdict is that the verse, because derivative and deracinative, cannot equal the music. "Rose read a second selection, a spasmodic, equally artificial graft, a supposedly deeply emotional lyric, an echo of Mrs. Browning, with a third line which went plumbing to the deeps of passion after a rhyme" (p. 241). The contrast between indigenous gifts and derivative attempts is a suggestive one, for it shows the missing dimension in Rose's poetry. The idiom and the matter of her homeplace on the Coolly must somehow be found in the city of Chicago.

When the city finally speaks to Rose concerning the country, the medium is Chicago's newest and proudest institution: the opera, housed in Louis Sullivan's architectural triumph, the Auditorium Theatre, but ironically presenting the artifacts of high European culture. Rose is the guest of a prominent social family in their loge and is titillated by the glittering society and the imposing building. But it is the music of Richard Wagner that constitutes the transforming experience:

> The voice of Wagner came to her for the first time, and shook her and thrilled her and lifted her into wonderful regions where the green trees dripped golden moss, and the grasses were jeweled in very truth. Wistful young voices rose above the lazy lap of waves, sad with love and burdened with beauty which destroyed. Like a deep purple cloud death came, slowly, resistlessly, closing down on those who sang, clasped in each other's arms.
>
> They lay dead at last, and up through the purple cloud their spirits soared like gold and silver flame, woven together, and the harsh thunder of the gray sea died to a sullen boom (p. 271).

The music is, of course, the "Love-death" from *Tristan and Isolde*, though Garland does not identify it, and the description of its program and power carries the reader, as it must have carried Rose, back to that first sexual experience amid the forests and streams of the Coolly, where the young girl had felt the ache of "something passing" as she loved for the first time. Could Wagner's romantic landscape somehow be the Coolly? It could indeed if the imaginative fusion took place in the mind of the poet. "All I have written is to-night trash!" Rose exclaims after the opera. The consciousness link between place and human character is in one transfiguring moment made complete. The mature sense of place in midwestern literature will be a reality in Rose Dutcher's new poetic voice. To be sure, it is but an implied voice, since Garland never offers the reader a single line of her Coolly poetry, and the artistic breakthrough in sense of place occurs in a putative book of verse written by a fictional character, and not in the novel *Rose of Dutcher's Coolly!* An admission of artistic inadequacy? Perhaps, but in any event the mysterious and undescribed transformation of the Coolly into the romantic art of place is Garland's way of passing the buck to the twentieth century: here is the program and the potential, take it where I was not able to venture.

The love, the grand passion Rose has all along been expecting, comes in the person of one Warren Mason—journalist, intellectual, social critic, and almost a novelist. His characterization is unfortunately too weak to satisfy, and the reader is forced to feel as if the masterful Rose Dutcher, so beautiful and mature at the end of the novel, is getting shortchanged. Possibly that was Garland's intent, though not apparent, to make Rose and his audience realize that "William de Lisle" can only be idealized in a girl's imagination and in a woman's poetry, but never in domestic existence or within the institution of marriage. Whatever the case of intent, the truth is that Rose is so large a character that both men in the novel are rather lugubrious in her presence. Neither Garland nor Warren Mason are really comfortable in Rose's world, and rather than have the clumsy lover intrude into the essential fineness of that world, we will allow him only a fleeting appearance in these pages on *Rose*.

The portrait of Rose Dutcher gave the midwestern fictional woman a new psychological reality, a new sense of intellectual and creative integrity and a different sensibility. *Rose of Dutcher's Coolly* attempted to show feminine freedom and sexual awareness as things positive and socially edifying, as qualities necessary for the mature culture Garland hoped the Middle Border would produce in time. It was an expansively optimistic vision, the basis for which lay in the vitalizing influence of the land: the succession of yeoman farms across the Coollys of Wisconsin. The family farm was dying, the farmers and their wives were drudges, but for the sons and daughters, especially the daughters, free as they were from the entailment of staying on the farms and bitterly awaiting the end, was there not something better in store? Their characters were formed on the life-affirming land, then fulfilled through deprovincializing experiences in the greater world, at college, and in the cities. The key was to avoid deracination, to keep at least imaginative continuity between country and city. This fictional program generated the best of all possible American characters: neither too narrow from unrelieved toil and inflexible frontier institutions, nor too diffuse and equivocal from an excess of urbanity. But like so much of Garland's vision it was a program not destined to prevail in American literature or life. *Main Street*'s Carol Kennicott suffocated when she tried to exercise the prerogatives which ought to have been her inheritance from Rose. And Sherwood Anderson's queer little women found naught that was liberating in sex. *Rose of Dutcher's Coolly* stands virtually alone in its hopeful attitude toward human growth among the women and men of the Midwest. In view of this, Hamlin Garland's achievement in his only distinguished novel is all the more remarkable.

NOTES—CHAPTER III

1. Hamlin Garland, *A Son of the Middle Border* (New York: Grosset and Dunlap, 1927), p. 371.
2. Garland, *Son of the Middle Border*, p. 415.
3. Garland, *Son of the Middle Border*, pp. 415–16.
4. A *coulee*, or *coolly*, is a kind of gulch or ravine, often dry in the summer, characteristic of the topography of southern Wisconsin.
5. See the discussion of Robert Herrick's *Memoirs of an American Citizen* below in Ch. V.
6. William Dean Howells, *Criticism and Fiction* (New York: New York University Press, 1959), p. 41.
7. Joseph Kirkland to Hamlin Garland, 23 May 1887, Kirkland Papers.
8. Joseph Kirkland to his family, 4 July 1887, Kirkland Papers.
9. Hamlin Garland, *Crumbling Idols* (Cambridge, Mass.: Harvard University Press, 1960), p. 30.
10. Garland, *Crumbling Idols*, p. 11.
11. "Among other proscribed books I read Whitman's *Leaves of Grass* and without doubt that volume changed the world for me as it did for many others.... I rose from that first reading with a sense of having been taken up into high places. The spiritual significance of America was let loose upon me" (Garland, *Son of the Middle Border*, p. 323). Garland no doubt also assimilated Whitman's impassioned essay on democratic literature, "Democratic Vistas" (1871).
12. From the Northwest Ordinance of 1787, which provided the governing structure for the Ohio Valley. The phrase has recently been adopted as the motto for *The Old Northwest*, a new "journal of regional life and letters," which is attempting to carry on the old mandate.
13. Garland, *Crumbling Idols*, p. 60.
14. Garland, *Crumbling Idols*, p. 143.

15. This section is adapted from an article in the summer 1976 issue of *The Great Lakes Review*, and used by permission.

16. Larzer Ziff, *The American 1890s* (New York: Viking Press, 1966), p. 103.

17. Hamlin Garland, *Rose of Dutcher's Coolly* (Lincoln: University of Nebraska Press, 1969), p. 17. Subsequent references are contained within the body of the essay.

18. Compare Garland's passage with this one from *The Awakening:* "The hot wind beating in my face made me think... of a meadow that seemed as big as the ocean to the very little girl walking through the grass, which was higher than her waist. She threw out her arms as if swimming when she walked, beating the tall grass as one strikes out in the water.... I could see only the green before me, and I felt as if I must walk on forever" (New York: Capricorn Books, 1964, pp. 41–42).

19. The best example in contemporary American literature is in the work of William Faulkner, in his Quentin Compsons and Darl Bundrens, characters for whom there can be no positive causal connection between past and present. This is the essence of modern literary tragedy, and is suggestively foreshadowed in the fate of Edna Pontellier in *The Awakening*, who finds the recollected image of her childhood romantic ideal (a touring tragedian) to be a demoralizing influence in her adult life.

20. Returning to the Middle Border after a three years' absence in Boston, Garland saw as with new eyes the murderous travails of western agrarian life. Everywhere he saw "beautiful youth becoming bowed and bent. I saw lovely girlhood wasting away into thin and hopeless age. Some of the women I had known had withered into querulous and complaining spinsterhood, and I heard ambitious youth cursing the bondage of the farm" (*Son of the Middle Border*, p. 365).

CHAPTER IV

The City of Money:
Henry Blake Fuller's Chicago

> To whom may the laurels as laureate of this Florence of the
> west yet fall? This singing flame of a city, this all America, this
> poet in chaps and buckskin, this rude, raw Titan, this Burns of
> a city! By its shimmering lake it lay, a kind of shreds and
> patches, a maundering yokel with an epic in its mouth, a
> tramp, a hobo among cities, with the grip of Caesar in its
> mind, the dramatic force of Euripides in its soul. A very bard
> of a city this, singing of high deeds and high hopes, its heavy
> brogans buried deep in the mire of circumstances.
>
> —Theodore Dreiser, *The Titan*

Money and Manners—*The Cliff-Dwellers*

Hamlin Garland's good friend, Henry Blake Fuller, was one of those
odd expatriates who kept coming home to Chicago despite an obvious
predilection for Europe, finally, in the early 1890s—with a sigh and a
shrug of the shoulders—settling down to business in the city for good.
Yet his Continental adventures had already made Fuller a writer,[1] and it
was natural for him to attempt to do something with Chicago: he was
there and he wished to continue his authorship, even as an avocation.
Hence he looked at the life around him and soon began polishing
Chicago's rough stones into fiction. He could never, of course, allow the
new Florence the rarefied cultural distinction of the old, but Chicago was
socially dynamic in a way unique to American cities of the day, and Fuller
sensed a literary potential that demanded to be drawn out. He began his
Chicago work, as he said, after "the Columbian Exposition helped along
a hearing for Chicago fiction,"[2] thus adding his name to the growing
roster of young writers attempting to take advantage of the national

91

interest in Chicago fostered by the fair. This new impetus for Fuller lasted only about three years, but it served as the motivation for a pair of fascinating novels, *The Cliff-Dwellers* (1893) and *With the Procession* (1895). Both works were well received—within the city and across the land—and helped make Henry Blake Fuller the principal literary delineator of the city during the important decade of the 1890s.

For a number of reasons *The Cliff-Dwellers* and *With the Procession* deserve to be taken together as a single statement of their author's sense of urban sociology. Beyond the obvious fact that they share a single setting, the novels have in common a studied interest in the social class they picture, namely the upwardly mobile business bourgeoisie of Chicago. And this similarity suggests another and a deeper one: the novels are part (the only part, unfortunately) of an abridged chronicle of Chicago, a chronicle more social than familial, of two books where half a dozen or so were needed. Fuller's novels focus on a localized social ambience, utterly complete and defined, in its own way as insular and provincial as anything in Kirkland's Spring County or Eggleston's Moscow. This is one way of saying that *The Cliff-Dwellers* and *With the Procession* are anything but panoramic, for Chicago considered as a total social universe awaited the different talents of the later naturalistic writers. Fuller's characters nearly always live within the respectable middle-class perimeters of Near South or Near North and, undeviating as accelerated particles, make their diurnal pilgrimages to and from the Loop, as this now-famous region was already beginning to be called in the 1890s. Newcomers appear within this limited circumference, are tried on for size, and either succeed or fail. No questions of qualification or origin are ever posed of the suppliant: except in the case of business failure, for business failure precipitates social failure. It is as simple as this. They come and go, in other words, and those who have stayed (and stayed rich) the longest, say upwards of one full generation, are accorded patrician status. No other criterion of worth is obvious in the "city on the lake on the make."

Henry Blake Fuller was one of the first American writers to discern the magic of money in American urban life. Not just the power, but the magic. Both of his Chicago novels are permeated with the presence of money, symbolized in mysterious Cecelia Ingles, who is not so much a character as an allegory. Cecelia Ingles, the social magic of name and position, for was she not wife to Arthur J. Ingles, builder and owner of the "Clifton," the skyscraper home of the entire tribe of "cliff-dwellers?" Cecelia Ingles, arbitress absolute of social visits and charity balls, whose presence is palpable, like a fatality, throughout both books. She is Fuller's frankly uncharacterized voice of the quixotic but nonetheless irresistible force of wealth. She is the literary ancestor of Scott Fitzgerald's Daisy Buchanan, for her voice too is "full of money," and the more portentously so as it is a disembodied voice. The idea that Chicago and Chicagoans were not only making but made of money received as careful an ethical analysis as Fuller could contrive. His agent on the money question was that rarest of sorts in Chicago (and in Chicago novels), an honest man. Theodore Brower, who appears in both novels, is not rich nor wishing he could get rich. He does, however, want to see some changes made in Chicago's money orientation. Brower speaks calmly but forcefully, with the kind of native intimacy and affection that can reduce an unwieldy melting pot of a million inhabitants to "this town of ours":

> This town of ours labors under one peculiar disadvantage: it is the only great city in the world to which all its citizens have come for the one common, avowed object of making money. There you have its genesis, its growth, its end and object; and there are but few of us who are not attending to that object very strictly. In this Garden City of ours every man cultivates his own little bed and his neighbor his; but who looks after the paths between? They have become a kind of No Man's Land, and the weeds of a rank iniquity are fast choking them up. The thing to teach the public is this: that the general good is a different thing from the sum of the individual goods.[3]

Possibly this was Fuller's greatest contribution to the literary outlook of the twentieth century, the acute insight that "money does the talking in American society, whoever may do the speaking."[4] Unlike Dreiser and Frank Norris, Fuller declined to be bowled over by the mystifying "Chicago spirit" that so impressed them, for behind the dynamic optimism and the raucous hoopla he sensed only the cynical and smirking silence of money.

Seen, then, as the initial volume in a Chicago sequence, *The Cliff-Dwellers* becomes the exploration of the city's topography—physical and social. The action involves the rise and fall of a certain subsection of the Chicago business community, the rich and the middling, the managers and the managed. If there is a focus, it is upon the fortunes (falling) and the character (rising) of young George Ogden, a transplanted New Englander in search of Chicago's spectacular "main chance." George Ogden is thrust into the center of things, and all these "things" are unified and given significance through the eighteen "soaring [stories] of brick and limestone and granite"[5]—steel skeletons being a year or so away—that constituted the Clifton building, the tallest in all of Chicago. The fictional Clifton is recognizably the august Monadnock, John Wellborn Root's austere triumph in masonry completed in 1891, which may still be seen standing like an old proud patriarch at the corner of Jackson and Dearborn in the Loop.[6] Fuller must have been as surprised as the rest of Chicago to watch the Monadnock reach higher and higher into the sky above an undeveloped area of the Loop full of "cheap one-story shacks" and "mere hovels."[7] Begun on the ragged edge of the business sector of the city, the Monadnock soon became the definitive symbol of Chicago's limitless social and economic aspirations.

Perhaps it occurred to Fuller, steeped as he was in European medievalism, that such aspirations were akin to the Gothic impulse, which sent its cathedral spires higher and higher toward heaven. But if so he could by no means bring himself to credit secular Chicago with so pure and selfless a purpose. When he chose a metaphor for the inhabitants of the tall buildings springing up around him it was laced with irony rather than awe. The perspicacity of this urban metaphor, developed conceitlike in the opening pages of *The Cliff-Dwellers,* has often been praised, and with justice. The ironic thrust compares the life within the buildings to that of the earlier civilization of the (extinct) cliff-dwellers of the Southwest: the Clifton somehow reminds Fuller of El Capitan and to his facetious eye the streets eighteen stories below run like "cañons," while the misty and unwholesome lake breezes recall the Bridal Veil at Yosemite.

> The explorer who has climbed to the shoulder of one of these great captains and has found one of the thinnest folds in the veil may readily make out the nature of the surrounding country. The ragged and erratic plateau of the Bad Lands lies before him in all its hideousness and impracticability. It is a wild tract full of sudden falls, unexpected rises, precipitous dislocations. The high and the low are met together. The big and the little alternate in a rapid and illogical succession. Its perilous trails are followed successfully by but few—by a lineman, perhaps, who is balanced on a cornice, by a roofer astride some dizzy gable, by a youth here and there whose early apprehension of the main chance and the multiplication table has stood him in good stead (pp. 2–3).

Here is more of a social landscape than a natural, with its "sudden falls" and "unexpected rises," so typically and damnably American, Fuller felt, in its "illogical succession" of big and little. Who would be on top of the Clifton tomorrow, having scaled its heights by the ropes and boots of the main chance? And perhaps more to the point, who will have taken a serious fall or worse? New as the landscape is, however, it smacks of institutional permanence in Chicago and in America, for the members of this unlikely tribe

> gather daily around their own great camp-fire. This fire heats the four big boilers under the pavement of the court which lies just behind, and it sends aloft a vast plume of smoke to mingle with those of other like communities that are settled round about. These same thousands may gather ... at their tribal feast, for the Clifton has its own lunch-counter just off one corner of the grand court, as well as a restaurant several floors higher up. The members of the tribe may also smoke the pipe of peace among themselves whenever so minded, for the Clifton has its own cigar stand just within the principal entrance. Newspapers and periodicals, too, are sold at the same place. The warriors may also communicate their messages, hostile or friendly, to chiefs more or less remote; for there is a telegraph office in the corridor and a squad of messenger-boys in wait close by (p. 5).

The Clifton is the prototype for George Babbitt's Reeves Building in the twentieth century (Sinclair Lewis's *Babbitt*, 1922), by which time the American businessman is securely and smugly encastled behind fortress-like walls.[8] Even in its spanking newness—newness of purpose and of architectural aspect—the Clifton was self-sufficient. "In a word, the Clifton aims to be complete within itself, and it will be unnecessary for us to go afield either far or frequently during the present simple succession of brief episodes in the lives of the Cliff-dwellers" (p. 5).

Who then were the fabulous cliff-dwellers? One, as we have seen, was the easterner George Ogden, who brought with him to Chicago more Brahmin pride than would do him good in a city where origins usually didn't count. Another was his quiet and steady friend Brower. Still another was the unscrupulous financier Erastus Brainard, who had managed by the agency of money to elevate his family in society, despite his shortcomings—recognized by all the cliff-dwellers—in the matter of business ethics. Brainard, we are given to understand, has a past:

> Brainard had come up from the southern part of the state—from "Egypt" as it is called. A darkness truly Egyptian brooded over his early history, so that if it is a fact that he was an exhorter at Methodist camp-meetings in his early twenties, proof of the fact might be sought in vain. The first definite point in his early career is this: that as a youngish man he was connected in some capacity with

a cross-country railroad on the far side of Centralia. How successful he was in transporting souls no one can say; that he has been successful in transporting bodies no one will deny. He is unrivalled in his mastery of the street-car question, and his operations have lain in many scattered fields (pp. 34–35).

It looks as if some of Eggleston's "poor whiteys" took to the city rather than to Pike County, sensing in places like Chicago another lawless frontier wherein they might work their unfettered wills with much more dramatic prospects. Erastus Brainard is the first of a long string of business heroes and villains who have risen from obscure and questionable rural backgrounds. In later years such characters as Robert Herrick's Van Harrington and Sherwood Anderson's Sam McPherson (*Windy McPherson's Son*, 1916) would regularly invade the city from the towns and farms of the country in search of both their fortune and an outlet for their predatory instincts. Brainard, with all the hypocrisy of a powerful prince, does not hesitate to try to ruin George Ogden when the "fallen" eastener is caught doing on an infinitesimal scale that which had made the financier rich. For a couple of hundred dollars' worth of embezzlement from Brainard's Underground National Bank (basement of the Clifton, of course), taken by Ogden to keep the wolf from the door after the disasters of his wife's expensive social climbing and subsequent lingering illness, the vindictive Brainard would drive the unfortunate young man back to Boston. "Nobody really knew who he was," Brainard says, in a vicious ironic inversion of the East's undemocratic insistence on pedigree and family connection. "He was put in a good place and he was pushed right along. Hasn't he ever guessed why?" (p. 290). The reason had been the tycoon's notion of further legitimizing his wealth by marrying his daughter Abbie to eastern respectability. But Ogden had chosen differently. Hence Brainard's wrath, born of class feeling, when Ogden steals from necessity. This was fighting under the Chicago rules, and George Ogden should have foreseen his utter defeat.

George and Abbie do eventually get together, but only after the deaths of his wife and her father. Their union required both the dissipation of the Brainard millions through mismanagement and the chastening of Ogden's eastern pride. The novel ends with the couple, now fully cognizant of what Fuller calls the "middlingness of their lot" (p. 323), watching an opera, not from a privileged loge but from a modest seat in the balcony. They notice that a certain box, vacant for two acts, has been claimed by a party of four. The tardy set includes Chicago's leading architect and his wife, along with Arthur J. Ingles, the supremely wealthy owner of the Clifton. "'And who is the other lady?'" asks Abbie. "'I—I have never seen her before,'" answers George, "but he knew perfectly well who she was. He knew that she was Cecelia Ingles, and his heart was constricted at the sight of her. It is for such a woman that one man builds a Clifton and that a hundred others are martyred in it" (p. 324). Ogden indeed has never seen Cecelia Ingles, though she is by the evidences of the society pages in the newspapers everywhere. The presence, the money, either appears for a brief and conspicuous third-act display or it does not grace the opera at all. Ogden's heart is "constricted" because he is one of the martyred hundred, his well-being destroyed by a naturalistic force not even to be seen, let alone comprehended. "A margin of wealth is helpful to civilization, but for some mysterious reason great wealth is destructive."[9] And a fortiori, one might say, when all the great wealth, or nearly all, is in the hands of the newly rich, who have yet to relax in the Chicago they created and let leisure humanize their fortunes. We see that George Ogden will live a life never quite free of the pain caused by his initial defeat in the city: his eastern values did not hold up sufficiently against the Chicago onslaught. And he represents the nameless thousands who came to the city and were immediately bewildered by its illogical alternation of "high and low," as Fuller put it. He failed to comprehend the essential nature of its social and commercial processes. Name, place, training—these meant little on the urban frontier if you succeeded, meant everything apparently if you failed. Ogden's expansive expectations for himself and his adopted city are brought crashing down by the novel's pessimism, but it is worth while recalling just what those expectations had been:

> "And the books that are coming in!" cried Jessie Ogden.... "Does the enemy know that four of the biggest buildings in this big city are built of books?"
>
> "The new libraries," her husband explained—"the ones that are going to make us the literary centre."
>
> "Dear me," said Winthrop, "are you expecting that?"
>
> "Oh, yes. And we expect to be the financial centre, and presently the political centre, too...."
>
> "And where is Boston?"
>
> "A little behind," said Fairchild. "New York is the main-mast yet. Chicago ranks as foremast—at present; while Boston is—"
>
> "The mizzen-mast," completed Ogden.
>
> "And we Chicago folks stand at the bow," chimed in his wife, "and sniff the first freshness of the breeze" (p. 241).

One of the lessons Fuller had learned in Europe was that civilization might not be created quite so fast, or merely by the collective will of American merchant princes. Such magic had not even been possible in the first Florence. Chicago might expect and get material splendor, as witness the Cliftons and the Monadnocks. But the question of a civilization for the city would have to be deferred until a time when the human population within these marvels of design and engineering ceased being martyrs, either collectively or individually, and were allowed simply to inhabit.

Money and Morality—*With the Procession*

Could the humanly destructive power of money be successfully opposed in the Chicago of the 1890s? The rather elaborate answer to this question provided the program for Fuller's second (and better) Chicago novel, *With the Procession* (1895). As the title suggests, once again Fuller found an urban metaphor large enough and dynamic enough to synthesize the whole of Chicago's social life. The procession, like the Clifton, does indeed help determine the directions of men's and women's lives, but it has a fluidity and a freedom beyond even the socialized art of a towering building: it is a procession, made up of the whole lot of mankind, an endless prospect of American Everyman too vast and diffuse to be directed by the wills of Cecelia and Arthur J. Ingles. No, Chicago hasn't changed, but Fuller's attitude has evolved, probably as he himself has settled in more authoritatively with his city. He had begun to make his accommodation with the procession, even as he was showing America a fictional solution to the urban problem of living and dealing decently with one's fellows amid the welter of seemingly incomprehensible change that constituted a typical year in Chicago. Henry Blake Fuller, out on the new urban frontier, was sloughing off his old and artistically precious skin, was democratizing and, in the best sense of the word, urbanizing: now it was the native American voice of William Dean Howells which called—look at the truth of "the worth of the vulgar," it urged; and the *pensieri vani* of the erstwhile expatriate became just that.

Fuller does not begin *With the Procession* with the procession, this time reserving the metaphor until his plot of manners is introduced. The novel both begins and ends with the dying and the death of old David Marshall, wholesale grocer and founder of an established Chicago family. The credentials of the Marshalls might be inferred from the fact that their solid old South Side home had not only been built before the Great Fire of 1871 but before the Civil War, built far enough out on Michigan Avenue to escape the scourge of the flames, yet sufficiently close in to maintain a kind of old-family respectability. But the Marshalls are socially out of practice as the novel opens. They are off to one side and in danger of being passed by, overrun by the insurgency of the newly rich, by the appearance of a new set of social and civic values and by the currency of "modern" business ethics which do not pause to honor the old Chicago families just because they are old. The Marshalls' position in society is anomalous and this is what ultimately does Father Marshall in. So long as he might go about the straightforward business of feeding thousands of Chicagoans he prospered and was content. But confronted with the painful image of his family consigned to the rear of the procession, he faltered.

When old Mr. Marshall finally took to his bed, the household viewed this action with more surprise than sympathy, and with more impatience than surprise. It seemed like the breaking down of a machine whose trustworthiness had been hitherto infallible; his family were almost forced to the acknowledgement that he was but a mere human being after all ... their dismay was now such as might occur at the Mint if the great stamp were suddenly and of its own accord to cease its coinage of double eagles and to sink into a silence of supine idleness ... poor old David Marshall was like one of the early Tuscan archangels, whose scattered members are connected by draperies merely, with no acknowledged organism within; nor were his shining qualities fully recognized until the resolutions passed by the Association of Wholesale Grocers reached the hands of his bereaved—
But this is no way to begin (p. 3).

It is precisely the way to begin, as Fuller well knows. His probing irony, if anything sharper than in *The Cliff-Dwellers*, suggests that David Marshall was in his day much, much more than a programmed money machine, though his family in their material demands has not been able to judge him fairly. This is to be the subject of *With the Procession:* the Marshall family's rediscovery—led by the eldest daughter, Jane—of their father's heritage and social worth, which knowledge they must then employ toward the end of a social reemergence. In other words the Marshalls must learn the lessons of the past before they can resume their rightful place in the procession of the present into the future. The courtship between Jane Marshall and Theodore Brower offers a convenient novel-of-manners basis upon which to build the drama of finding for the Marshall family, once again, a just ethical accommodation with the immense and ongoing procession.

The American social procession turns out to have its urban correlative in an actual procession of traffic in downtown Chicago. It is noisy and anxious, full to straining with all kinds of folk going in every different direction.

> The grimy lattice-work of the drawbridge swung to slowly, the steam-tug blackened the dull air and rolled the turbid water as it dragged its schooner on towards the lumber-yards of the South Branch, and a long line of waiting vehicles took up their interrupted course through the smoke and the stench as they filed across the stream into the thick of business beyond; first a yellow street-car; then a robust truck laden with rattling sheet-iron, or piled high with fresh wooden pails and willow baskets; then a junk-cart bearing a pair of dwarfed and bearded Poles, who bumped in unison with the jars of its clattering springs; then, perhaps, a bespattered buggy, with reins jerked by a pair of sinewy and impatient hands. Then more street-cars; then a butcher's car loaded with carcasses of calves—red, black, piebald—or an express wagon with a yellow cur yelping from its rear; then, it may be, an insolently venturesome landau, with crested panel and top-booted coachman. Then drays and omnibuses and more street-cars; then, presently, somewhere in the line, between the tail end of one truck and the menacing tongue of another, a family carry-all—a carry-all loaded with its family, driven by a man of all work, and encumbered with baggage which shows the labels of half the hotels of Europe (p. 4).

Fuller's "perhaps's" and "it may be's" emphasize the typicality of this sort of traffic procession: it happens many times a day in Chicago. And the goodly smattering of hyphenated words attests the dynamic novelty of urban American society, as the wordsmiths struggle to hammer out new nouns to describe the welter. It is quite a procession, and rival cities would have to "go some" to get ahead of Chicago.

And there, to the rear and obscured by the rush and the press, are the Marshalls. The youngest son, Truesdale Marshall, has at long last returned home (though begrudgingly) from a protracted grand tour on the Continent, and the family, having ventured out to meet him, is in danger of being overwhelmed. Yet the Chicago rule is that all must travel in the procession, and so there they are in their out-of-fashion carry-all. To Fuller the rattle of worn wheels seems to say, "I am not of the great world ... I make no pretense to fashion. We are steady and solid, but we are not precisely in society.... However, do not misunderstand our position; it is not that we are under, nor that we are exactly aside; perhaps we have been left just a little behind" (p. 5). In *With the Procession* money is talking more loudly than ever, it seems, and Fuller in a delightfully contemporary anticipation of the argot of conspicuous consumption spoken by the American automobile puts words in the mouth of the carry-all. "How are they to catch up again," Fuller asks, "how rejoin the great caravan whose fast and furious pace never ceases, never slackens?" (p. 5).

Society has one program for catching up, Fuller another. According to the former the Marshalls must make certain prescribed social and civic gestures: the children must have a belated coming out and the parents—particularly the father David Marshall—must ... well, they must build things. There must be a magnificent new many-storied office building for the firm of Marshall and Belden; there must be a fashionable new residence for the family further out on Michigan Avenue, preferably one built by Chicago's most popular architect, Tom Bingham; and David Marshall must underwrite a hall to immortalize the family name on the campus of the new university. Now to Fuller this was all dangerously wrongheaded, and in *With the Procession* he continues the theme initiated in the earlier novel: the human waste attendant on building cultural and social monuments for their own sake, and once again the architecture dominating the landscape is a negative environmental force, because it lacks the democratic human measure. For Fuller, in the ethical as well as the architectural sense, "form followed function," and a building's function was to provide a decent living for its occupants.

The travails involved in the negotiating, planning, and executing of these Marshall family showpieces occupy most of the novel, and their ultimate failure demonstrates Fuller's suspicions about the efficacy of a social initiation that extracts such a high human price. For the buildings end up causing great pain for the Marshalls. The plans hang like millstones around the neck of Jane, who does the most to further their building, though she cannot deeply affirm the whole thing. One by one, the buildings prove more or less abortive: the house turns out to be nothing at all like their previous home, the new office building is never topped out due to the financial failure of Marshall, Belden, and Company, and the college building has its bequest removed by a convenient codicil to David Marshall's will. It is obvious that Fuller's stipulations for reentering the procession are far different from society's. He would have the family learn the lessons of their old-Chicago past in order to reject any practice of pecuniary emulation of the upstart rich around them. It is a question of

101

rediscovering the mode of decent living which has traditionally surrounded Chicago's monied class. And Jane Marshall begins to be en-
lightened when she becomes the protégé of Susan Granger Bates.

The portrait of Mrs. Bates is perhaps Fuller's most charming creation,
and one of the best characterizations in all of Chicago fiction. The initial
meeting between Jane and Mrs. Bates is designed as a kind of confronta-
tion between the younger woman's rather naive "Hull House" liberalism
and Susan Bates's aristocratic social distance. The lesson for Jane is how
utterly wrong she can be about some rich folks. She calls upon Mrs. Bates
to ask for a contribution to one of her pet social-welfare projects, a
proposed lunch club for Loop working girls. Jane begins inauspiciously
enough: instead of invoking the Marshall family name, which she wrong-
ly thinks without social weight, Jane drops the name of her aunt, who is
an obscure social pretender. Mrs. Bates is predictably unmoved. Jane is
mortified. But coldness is manifestly what she deserves for so widely mis-
construing both the relative social status of her own family and the kind
of approach that might work with a woman like Susan Granger Bates.
The scene is reminiscent of Garland's Rose's performance in the offices
of Dr. Isabel Herrick, and both girls' response to their ill-met overtures is
anger and panic. But of course when Mrs. Bates discovers Jane's true
family connections all is suddenly made right: "Mrs. Bates seized Jane's
unwilling hands. She gathered those poor, stiff, knotted fingers into two
crackling bundles within her own plump and warm palms, squeezed them
forcibly, and looked into Jane's face with all imaginable kindness. 'I had
just that temper once myself,' she said" (p. 45). Behold within the inner-
most private circle of the Chicago aristocracy a person who is just plain
folks, or at least used to be. Mrs. Bates turns out to be a self-made
woman in the same sense that her husband, a great financier, is a self-
made man. The daughter of poor parents, a veteran of self-reliant but
menial domestic service, several years as a schoolmarm, then marriage followed by the mythical steady upward rise of the Bates' fortunes, with
Susan at all times the proverbial woman behind the man. This was the
nutshell history of her life as she breathlessly related it to an astonished
Jane Marshall. It is the familiar Horatio and Alice Alger story, dressed up
and given artistic interest by the wit and powers of characterization of
Henry Blake Fuller.

To accompany the rags-to-riches rehearsal, Mrs. Bates gives Jane a
tour of the opulent family mansion, but not just any tour: the two of
them wander from room to room, looking for a nook where they can chat
as friends and escape the awesome amplitude of the luxury. One senses

that even Susan Bates is not especially comfortable amid the conspicuous display. They find no friendly place in the music room, de rigeur with grand piano and large folio scores; nor in the library with its rows of leathern classics ("Sets—sets—sets," Mrs. Bates remarks in despair, p. 49); certainly not in the Grand Salon, all glittering excess of Louis Quinze; and not in the Gallery, where the might-be Corot occupies the central place ("that morning thing over there is a Corot—at least, we think so. I was going to ask one of the French commissioners about it last summer [during the Columbian Exposition], but my nerve gave out at the last minute. Mr. Bates bought it on his own responsibility. I let him go ahead, for, after all, people of our position would naturally be expected to have a Corot," p. 57). Not, in short, in any of the public places where the Bateses regularly have to defend their title as Chicago's premier social arbiters—vying with the ubiquitous Ingleses for that honor. Fuller is having more than a little fun with Mrs. Bates, as the irony of the "Corot" business so neatly demonstrates. But she is not destined in Fuller's hands to be either a silly or an evil representative of vulgar wealth, despite the obvious pride she takes in their accomplishment:

"There!" she said; "you've seen it all." She stood there in a kind of impassioned splendor, her jewelled fingers shut tightly and her fists thrown out and apart so as to show the veins and cords of her wrists. "*We* did it, we two—just Granger and I. Nothing but our own hands and hearts and hopes, and each other. We have fought the fight—a fair field and no favor—and we have come out ahead. And we shall stay there, too; keep up with the procession is my motto, and head it if you can. I *do* head it, and I feel that I'm where I belong. When I can't foot it with the rest, let me drop by the wayside and the crows have me. But they'll never get me—never! There's ten more good years in me yet; and if we were to slip to the bottom to-morrow, we should work back to the top again before we finished" (p. 58).

Notice that there is nothing distinctively urban about this rugged and mostly healthy individualism. It might be Zury Prouder boasting. And of course the Bateses had worked their way up from the country to the city, with the outcome spectacularly more successful than even the most optimistic paradigm had forecast.

Fuller lets Mrs. Bates get away with her enthusiastic but unregenerate materialism because she is a kind of natural, wholly unselfconscious about her vast wealth—accumulated fairly, it is stressed, and used mainly as the means to living rather than as life itself. Hers is not a position, he seems to be saying, that can stand any rigorous ethical analysis, but it is infinitely preferable to Chicago's newer and more vulgar wealth. Behind the ostentation thought necessary for public consumption stand a pair of plain old settlers. How extenuating is that simple fact in *With the Procession.* Thirty or forty years in Chicago would serve as three or four centuries in Europe. Mrs. Bates is a woman who can recall with relish the old neighborhood folk evenings, ebullient with squaredancing to the tune of "Old Dan Tucker." Now she might have a little gem of a landscape by Camille Corot hanging in her house. Yet Fuller is as gentle toward her as she toward Jane. Reminding the girl of her own old-family origins—for the Marshalls had been among the families who went to wingdings instead of charity balls—Mrs. Bates gently suggests that "perhaps you have not done your father justice" (p. 51), and Jane is forced to admit the truth of this penetrating observation. And in misjudging her father she inevitably has mistaken herself. "I took you at first for your father's sake," Mrs. Bates candidly remarks, "and kept you for your own. It's a long time since I have met a girl like you; I didn't suppose there was one left in the whole town. You are one of *us*—the old settlers, the aborigines" (p. 65). And so they sit down at that imposing grand piano and knock out a verse or two of "Old Dan'l," just for old times' sake and to assure themselves that the procession hasn't moved all that far after all. Thus this memorable scene ends: on a note recalling Garland's Rose, with her country culture, whistling in the urban dark of Chicago and somehow making it better. There is really nothing much in all of Chicago writing to prefer over this fourth chapter of *With the Procession.*

But the Marshalls discover they cannot emulate the Bateses, though Jane tries gamely enough. First she engineers her conceited little sister's coming out, aided and abetted of course by Susan Bates; then she leads the fight for the new Marshall residence, overcoming the inertia of her mother; and it is Jane who persuades her father to reenter the business-club world after a long hiatus. But none of these things works out, none brings the requisite happiness, and Jane finds herself faced, near the end of the novel, with a general family collapse. The business is dying, David Marshall is dying, Mrs. Marshall is demoralized, Truesdale is disgraced by the scandal of one of his European love affairs, little sister Rose is hopelessly infatuated with all the wrong things, and Jane—Jane is getting older. Enter at this crucial juncture one Theodore Brower, who declares himself just in time to save her from an emotional breakdown. Brower has been, throughout the novel, a family friend and advisor (he is in fact the same Theodore Brower who befriended George Ogden in *The Cliff-*

Dwellers), and he is the only character among them who actually lives and works among the people of the city. Brower is obviously an ethical center in *With the Procession,* a man firmly grounded in the social reality of life among the great many and therefore able to serve as a kind of moral referee in the painful transactions of the Marshalls with the different levels of Chicago society. But, interestingly enough, even Brower has a lesson to learn about the rich, for whom he has long entertained a quiet sort of scorn. At the earnest request of Jane, he escorts her to the annual Charity Ball, though, as Fuller humorously puts it, "he would immensely have preferred to pass the same length of time staring into a locomotive head-light" (pp. 144–45). Brower ends up promenading conspicuously with Mrs. Bates, who lectures him on the misapprehension, so widely held among the liberal young, that Chicago high society is full of "social butterflies." Indeed, according to her they are nearly as scarce as unicorns. But there is one ... "'It's Mrs. Ingles; you must meet her.' 'Some other time, please,' implored Brower" (pp. 145–46). The frightening natural-istic presence of *The Cliff-Dwellers* is here reduced to being merely a "but-terfly," dismissed by those like Mrs. Bates who are serious about reform-ing society. And Brower—what has he heard from George Ogden?—refuses the embarrassment of meeting the woman who used to do so much human damage. Susan Bates, however, is confident she can handle Cecelia Ingles. "I'm going to take her in hand pretty soon and make a good, earnest woman out of her" (pp. 145–46), and by so doing neutral-ize one of the last negative influences on the overall quality of the proces-sion: a dramatic shift in outlook from the gloom of *The Cliff-Dwellers.*

Theodore Brower, while assembling the courage to ask for Jane's hand, manfully tries to help the other Marshalls with their problems. He futilely tries to get a cynical and deracinated Truesdale interested in something, and just as futilely spends long evenings attempting to coax old man Marshall out of his despondent moods—moods brought on by David Marshall's realization that he, even more than the rest of his fami-ly, has been passed by. We see in father and son two social types who cannot reasonably hope to rejoin the procession. Truesdale because he was never in it during his own formative years, and father Mar-shall because he misanthropically stayed aloof too long before deigning to return.

But Brower has more to do than this. He principally serves as a foil to the character of Tom Bingham, Chicago's hottest and most fashionable architect,[10] who also happens to be Jane's most energetic and flamboyant suitor. How can Theodore Brower, fire-insurance investigator and Settlement House worker, hope to compete equally with the flashy architect? He wins the courtship race precisely because the ethical universe of the novel cannot allow Bingham, a "monument-minded man," to triumph. Bingham had been the one to convince David Marshall to donate the college hall and it was he who had from the first rather flatteringly encouraged Jane in her dreams for the new Marshall mansion. He is portrayed as the very self-interested booster for Chicago's civic building fad. "I was surprised, myself, to learn how many diverse opportunities this town offers.... People may preside at banquets ... and address public meetings, and head subscription papers, and found public baths, and build and endow colleges. And there are others who donate telescopes, or erect model lodging-houses, or set up statues and fountains" (p. 132). Be a Yerkes, a Wieboldt, or a Palmer, Bingham seems to be urging, and let me have the building of your immortality.[11] Brower supplants Bingham because the former is not a man who can unthinkingly affirm Chicago's mad rush toward physical completion. Generating public buildings for a public not even well understood by the patrician builders was to Theodore Brower a cruel inversion of social priorities. But at the end of the novel Jane Marshall vows, with Brower's acquiescence, to put David Marshall's money into a hall nonetheless. Even if it were to be built by the likes of Bingham, it should not be the same building as had been previously conceived. The hard lessons of experience and their joined social awareness would now be going into its very foundations. This alone was the proper kind of public gesture: a sacrifice rather than a celebration.

Henry Blake Fuller's achievement in his two Chicago novels is an impressive one. His artistry went beyond irony of expression and a glib style. He knew a resonant symbol when he saw one, and was able to ground it convincingly, even in the hectic material flux of turn-of-the-century Chicago. Fuller had the great (and all too rare) literary gift of the subsuming figure, and it allowed him to epitomize his Chicago society in the metaphors of the Clifton and the procession. *The Cliff-Dwellers* is organized around a metaphor of containment at best and entrapment at worst, and the disturbing prospect of the world within the new-fangled building sets the darkening tone of the entire novel. The procession, on the other hand, calls up both an image of Whitman's vast democratic vistas and the resilient and indefinite extent of William Dean Howells's American middle class. We prefer the procession to the Clifton because of its expansive possibilities for personal and national fulfillment. Mark Harris, a contemporary novelist with concerns not all that dissimilar to Fuller's, has written of *With the Procession* in words particularly apt to the purposes of this essay in rediscovery: "Conceivably, the Procession is the best of all possible processions, neither so ominous nor so destructive as we may fear. All that is finally certain is that Fuller, having described the conflict of values for himself in his own decades, describes it as well for us in ours. Few literary restorations are more to the present point."[12]

NOTES—CHAPTER IV

1. The fruits of his European years, as a kind of sentimental pilgrim in France and Italy, were *The Chevalier of Pensieri Vani* (1890) and *The Chatelaine of La Trinité* (1892).
2. Quoted in Constance Griffin, *Henry Blake Fuller, a Critical Biography* (Philadelphia: University of Pennsylvania Press, 1939), p. 19.
3. Henry Blake Fuller, *With the Procession*, ed. Mark Harris (Chicago: University of Chicago Press, Phoenix Books, 1966), p. 203. Subsequent references are contained within the body of the essay.
4. Ziff, *American 1890s*, p. 111.
5. Henry Blake Fuller, *The Cliff-Dwellers* (1893; reprint ed., Ridgewood, N.Y.: Gregg Press, 1968), p. 1. Subsequent references are contained within the body of the essay.
6. The architectural flowering of Chicago, 1880–1910, was one of the greatest cultural phenomena in the history of American art, and many of the buildings that fascinated Chicago writers and were employed by them as both realistic and symbolic settings in their fiction are still standing—perhaps considerably more begrimed than they were in the 1890s but otherwise outwardly the same as they looked at their creation. The best history of the building of the period is Carl Condit's *The Chicago School of Architecture* (Chicago: University of Chicago Press, 1964); the most thorough graphic record of the city's physical growth is Harold M. Mayer's and Richard C. Wade's *Chicago: Growth of a Metropolis* (Chicago: University of Chicago Press, 1969); the University of Chicago Press has also published, for "walkers and gawkers" like myself, *Chicago's Famous Buildings* (2d ed., 1969), in convenient guidebook size and format.
7. Condit, *Chicago School of Architecture*, p. 66.
8. The walls of the Monadnock were six feet thick at their base, and though this was necessary to support the immense weight of its sixteen stories, the walls remind one of the huge earth-and-masonry bases of old European fortresses, just as the massive Romanesque granite ground floor of Root's Rookery Building (Adams and LaSalle) suggests a new order of commercial building, one capable of withstanding long siege in the romantic business wars of high capitalism.
9. Kenneth Clark, *Civilisation* (New York: Harper and Row, 1969), p. 253.
10. Possibly modeled upon Daniel Burnham, of the firm of Burnham and Root, the builder of the White City of the Exposition and the designer of the ambitious "Plan of Chicago" (1909).

11. Charles Yerkes, financier and streetcar magnate, was fictionalized in Theodore Dreiser's *The Titan* (1914) as Frank Cowperwood, the "I-please-myself" neofeudal business lord whose social and political power was immense in the Chicago of the 1890s. Cowperwood-Yerkes is depicted as donating the famous University of Chicago Yerkes Observatory not as a philanthropist or public benefactor, but in order to convince Chicago banks to extend his credit!

12. In the preface to the edition of *With the Procession* I have used, p. xiv.

CHAPTER V

The City of Will:
Robert Herrick's Chicago [1]

> Chicago is an instance of a successful, contemptuous disregard
> of nature by man. Other great cities have been called gradually
> into existence about some fine opportunity suggested by
> nature, at the junction of fertile valleys, or on a loving bend of
> a broad river, or in the inner recesses of a sea-harbour, where
> nature has pointed out, as it were, a spot favourable for life
> and growth. In the case of Chicago, man has decided to make
> for himself a city for his artificial necessities in defiance of
> every indifference displayed by nature.
>
> —*The Gospel of Freedom*[2]

The Web of Life (1900)

When Robert Herrick came westward to the new University of
Chicago in the fall of 1893, drawn thither by the vigorous recruiting of
William Rainey Harper, who had raided the Harvard faculty the previous
spring and had picked up young Herrick in the process,[3] he could have
had no idea that he would remain in Chicago for thirty years. For at heart
he was a New England Mugwump, and the burgeoning city on Lake
Michigan was in all senses an alien landscape to him. Through the years
he never really learned to love his adopted city, though tolerate it he
might. And in his Chicago-based fiction he carried on a long war of attri-
tion with the city, getting more hostile reviews in the sensitive local press
with each succeeding novel that escalated his attack on Chicago's systematic ugliness. Particularly in a trio of novels—*The Web of Life* (1900),
The Common Lot (1904), and *The Memoirs of an American Citizen*
(1905)—Herrick worked out his two reflexive themes of Chicago life:

the city itself was made by the wrong sort of men for the wrong reasons, and the wrong sort of men continued to be made by the humanly unhealthy influence of the city.

In nearly every novel he wrote, Herrick stressed the need for individual ethical initiative, personal freedom, direct opposition to the dehumanizing tendencies of industrialization. Perhaps in other circumstances he might have taken a different city for his scene, but Chicago happened to be at hand and Chicago fascinated—however much an outsider he may have felt himself in its relentless hurly-burly. When Herrick arrived in Chicago, he did so (as had Hamlin Garland) at the height of the fair fever, a distemper that was promoting all manner of optimism about the future of Chicago and America; and, as Herrick's chief biographer has noted, he was caught up in the expansive mood of the day:

> For Herrick, the Fair, no less than the new University, gave expression to an emerging cultural vitality that promised well for the future of Chicago: "The Fair in a way was Chicago, its dream, its ideal, its noblest self incarnated...." He was moved, as Henry Adams and so many other visitors were moved, by its spiritual significance. "It was the fete day of our world, the big backbone of America, when it proclaimed to everybody that in spite of all the waste and ugliness and makeshift character of its civilization it had preserved its love of the ideal."[4]

Yet besides being slavishly derivative in its architecture the fair was ephemeral and evanescent; its plasterboard palaces would begin to vanish soon after the last visitor had passed out through the turnstiles. But would its impressive "spiritual significance" prove more durable, or was the infectious idealism to be as transient as the flimsy White City itself?

Robert Herrick answered this question to his own satisfaction in the Chicago novels he wrote over a period of almost two decades following the 1893 World's Columbian Exposition. There is in all of this work a forceful ethical strain, akin to the popular social fiction of the first Roosevelt era, but finer and more reverberant because Herrick was a better novelist than the popular Progressive writers. He scrupulously avoided the "formulas for reform" that were so central to the fiction of such writers as Joseph Medill Patterson, Booth Tarkington, and Brand Whitlock. He was perhaps the last gifted American novelist to study the changing national society in the manner of William Dean Howells—the last, that is, to study the subtleties of viable individual movement within a middle-class milieu that was by 1893 turning out to be more complex and more artistically suggestive than had previously been apparent. In one of the last of his Chicago novels, Herrick was to have his spokesman proclaim, at the end of the period of social hopefulness engendered by the fair, "The great end cannot come through political action, by theory or programme, by any division of the spoils, and readjustment of laws, but only by Will—the individual good will."⁵ For Herrick the question of America's spiritual health depended on the quality of the individual persons nurtured within her astonishing environments. And it is the city, in the Chicago novels, that supplies the ground for a kind of "American test case": whither the will? In his Chicago trio Herrick follows the will first with hope, then with doubt, and finally with undisguised sarcasm— the final attitude born of years of brooding watchfulness over a Chicago he came to know thoroughly but which he could never affirm.

The subtitle of *The Web of Life* might have been "After the Fair Is Over." The book traces the moral development of Howard Sommers, a young physician who quickly becomes disgusted with the venality and class-pandering of his profession and opts for a life of service and personal freedom. Sommers's ethical choices involve a conscious rejection of "his own," and Herrick injects a large amount of social criticism into the novel. But the distinctive achievement of *The Web of Life* is its remarkable integration of the action with the Chicago scene. The young doctor's alienation from his class parallels the course of Chicago's general disillusionment: the magnificent promise of the fair is tested against the real deprivation of late 1893, wavers in the face of mass human need, and is annihilated in the Fourth of July rioting at Pullman. Howard Sommers is on the scene for all of these events, an acute observer, even a participant on the periphery, and from them he gains spiritual insight: the social disintegration of Chicago is proof of the "big lie" character of the exposition and all it symbolized, for the fair was nothing more than a gaudy extrapolation of the status quo, and only of certain of its more pleasant features at that. And the entire dramatic structure of *The Web of Life* is based on this pattern of an individual's moral rise amidst the social decay of an entire city.

Several chapters into the novel, Howard Sommers says farewell to Louise Hitchcock, proud daughter of wealth and the woman he should be courting, at his last country club party: he is going back to the heart of the city, back to the vital drama of Pullman, the workers, and Alves Preston—a woman who will love him lucrative practice or no, love him the more because love is all they shall have. This casting off of class is the climactic scene in a series of encounters with the privileged classes that

111

convince Sommers there is something fundamentally wrong with the social contract, insofar as it applies to the huge majority of Chicagoans. He had first got into trouble among the managers and the financiers and their polite and silent wives by asking an inopportune question about the Pullman situation (the scene was a Hitchcock dinner party): "Is it so ... that the men who had been thrifty enough to get homes outside of Pullman had to go first because they didn't pay rent to the company?"[6] Sommers shows his temerity in probing the motives of the plutocrats, whose first-generation wealth has not yet had the leisure to liberalize itself and instead remains wholly predatory. Brome Porter, a director of the Pullman Palace Car Company, is quick to catechize Sommers in the dogmas of the neofeudal American business philosophy.

> The laborer has got some hard lessons to learn. This trouble is only a small part of the bigger trouble. He wants to get more than he is worth. And all our education, the higher education, is a bad thing.... That's why I wouldn't give a dollar to any begging college—not a dollar to make a lot of discontented, lazy duffers who go round exciting workingmen to think they're badly treated. Every dollar given a man to educate himself above his natural position is a dollar given to disturb a society.[7]

This antidemocratic cant is spoken by the same Brome Porter who near the end of the novel forces a stock market panic—seriously harming the Hitchcocks, his hosts, in the process—through one of his huge speculative swindles. Howard Sommers recognizes in himself a smoldering hatred of this sort of exploitative success. "I feel that way," he observes to Louise Hitchcock (who herself "hates views" in just the conventional way a young American woman of leisure ought), "pretty much all the time in America" (p. 40). Even so he temporizes with his conscience by joining the fashionable medical firm of Dr. Lindsay and for a time plays the game of "when in Chicago" by charging fat fees to suitably rich and hypochondriac women, as an alternative to a country or hospital practice among the people. But it is a foregone conclusion that he shall not be happy in his early choice.

During his internship, Sommers had become friends with Alves Preston after operating on her husband, and their intimacy grows toward love as she becomes the audience for his acrid expressions of personal dissatisfaction. He tells her, "I am a coward and conventional. I have learned to do as the others do. Medicine and education.... They are the two sciences where men turn and turn and emit noise and do nothing. The doctor and the teacher learn a few tricks and keep on repeating them as the priest does the ceremony of the mass" (p. 99). The earnest young physician is in the untenable position of needing very much to exercise his critical intellectual faculties in a society that does not recognize the critical instinct (or, as Thorstein Veblen put it, the instinct of workmanship) as a viable substitute for the acquisitive. On the Chicago scene of the 1890s how, exactly, does a man with no inclination for the predatory money game express himself? This was by no means only a fictional dilemma. It was daily faced by Herrick himself—Sommers's indicting irony spills over from medicine into the teaching profession—and by other of his University of Chicago colleagues, such as the poet William Vaughn Moody and the seminal social critic and theorist, Thorstein Veblen. Their traditional role in society was to act as efficacious moral agents, as sorters-out and patchers-up of the social mechanism. But what if nobody seemed to respect such work? The professions were either being ignored by the society at large or, what was worse, even being subverted by the new marching tunes of the Philistines. When one speaks of Robert Herrick as a New England Mugwump, this sort of professional powerlessness is what lies behind the term.[8] Very early in the novel Herrick gives Sommers an intuition that his only hope lies in the rejection of the medicine of affluence and a personal devotion to the medicine of healing. And the events of the novel help push him ever closer to this radical commitment. He had taken his degree in a springtime of promise. Now, as he makes his way up the North Shore to that last country club affair portending the conclusive break with the polo set, Sommers observes Chicago in the throes of a stifling summer, a correlative both of its economic depression and his own oppressed spirit:

> These days there were many people on the streets, but few were busy. The large department stores were empty; at the doors stood idle floor-walkers and clerks. It was too warm for the rich to buy, and the poor had no money. The poor had come lean and hungry out of the terrible winter that followed the World's Fair. In that beautiful enterprise the prodigal city had put forth her utmost strength, and, having shown the world the supreme flower of her energy, had collapsed. There was gloom, not only in LaSalle Street where people failed, but throughout the city, where the engine of play had exhausted the forces of all. The city's huge garment was too large for it; miles of empty stores, hotels, flat-buildings, showed its shrunken state. Tens of thousands of human beings, lured to the festive city by abnormal wages, had been left stranded, without food or a right to shelter in its tenant-less buildings (p. 135).

This sort of social situation is pregnant with potential reaction, and Howard Sommers, too, is ready for some fundamental change in his unhappy life. "Capital was sullen, and labor violent. There were meetings and counter-meetings: agitators, panaceas, university lecturers, sociologizing preachers, philanthropists, politicians—discontent and discord. The laborer starved, and the employer sulked" (pp. 135–36). No sooner is Sommers arrived in the gardenlike northern suburbs, sanctuaries from all reminders of the inner-city depression, than the threshold of his tolerance for the Dr. Lindsays, the Brome Porters, even the Louise Hitchcocks, is reached and passed. He realizes at this point that Chicago, despite the human horror of the Depression of '94, is life; the North Shore is simply the ultimate deracination, though it is but a short hour's ride by train. But what if the trains no longer run? This is precisely what happens, of course. The trains are stalled by Eugene Debs and his American Railway Union, leaving the deracinated either helplessly in or out of the city. Chicago, Sommers discerns, was made quickly, badly. Get out of it, yet keep on returning to gouge from it the continued means of getting away—the urgency of this cultural dilemma, so familiar for so long in urban America, sweeps Sommers back into Chicago, and not just into the Loop (he resigns from Lindsay's clinic) but into the heart of the city's neighborhoods. And very soon he is responding to all the variegated harmonics and overtones of the real Chicago:

> Decay, defeat, falling and groaning; disease, blind doctoring of disease; hunger and sorrow and sordid misery; the grime of living here in Chicago in the sharp discords of this nineteenth century; the brutal rich, the brutalized poor; the stupid good, the pedantic, the foolish,—all, all that make the waking world of his experience! It was like the smoke wreath above the lamping torch of the blast furnace. It was the screen upon which glowed the rosy colors of the essential fire. The fire,—that was the one great thing,—the fire was life itself (p. 167).

And on the Fourth of July, 1894, just before the Pullman rioting begins, the abandoned buildings of the White City go up in flames. Sommers and Alves Preston are two of the observers of this last ritual extinction of the fair's idealism before the holocaust of the embattled strikers against the Pullman management and the troops of the United States Government.[9] In the ensuing conflict of "them and us," Sommers finds himself squarely among the ranks of the despised "them": "He was not sorry for the change, so far as he had thought of it. At least he should escape the feeling of irritation, or criticism, which Lindsay so much deplored, that had been growing ever since he had left hospital work. The body social was diseased, and he could not make any satisfactory diagnosis of the evil; but at least he should feel better to have done with the privileged assertive classes, to have taken up his part with the less Philistine, more pitiably blind mob" (p. 194).[10]

In the heat of the summer labor battles and amidst the ruins of the White City, Sommers and Alves Preston consummate their love. But common-law marriage and people's medicine do not constitute the end of the moral development of the doctor. The two lovers suffer through a couple of years of subsistence, she teaching, he taking whatever cases offer. In Alves Preston Herrick created an intensely romantic character who gives her all for love in a credible way, and, when love does not prove to be all, just as believably withdraws from Sommers's life through suicide. She had lived their experiment in bohemian idealism to the fullest—love and love alone in the rent-free Greco-Roman ticket booth that was their home, a forlorn vestige of the White City which they occupied by a kind of urban squatters' rights. Her uncompromising commitment to the romantic ideal serves to reveal Sommers's own reactive position. He had come to her as he had come to the "people": on the rebound from an inarticulate and impotent rage against privilege. She realizes this much sooner than he, and it is she who breaks the bond between them: "I ruin the world for you. Love is not all,—at least for a man,—and somehow with me you cannot have the rest and love. We were wrong to rebel—I was wrong to take my happiness. I longed so! I have been so happy!" (p. 306).

Alves Preston in death "bade him go back to that fretwork, unsolvable world of little and great ... the vast web of petty greeds and blind efforts. He should return, but humbly, with the crude dross of his self-will burnt out" (pp. 315–16). Herrick does not accuse his protagonist of having been wrong about the essential nature of American society; rather he indicates that Howard Sommers has misconceived his own place in it. In his headlong initial reaction against the evils of unenlightened wealth, Sommers had rushed past, without noticing it, that crucial middle ground of American life. Now the average was all that was left him, both extremes having been ruled out through painful experience. This is Robert Herrick at his closest to the Progressives, but closer yet to Howells, who had his Basil Marches and Silas Laphams seek out their rightful province the hard way, and always located that province somewhere in the vast land of the American average. In the aftermath of love, social turmoil, and suicide, Sommers finds that "already Alves had bequeathed him something of herself. She had returned him to his fellow-laborers with a new feeling toward them, a humbleness he had never known, a desire to adjust himself with them" (p. 330). *Adjust* is the important word. The doctor is reentering society, not high society, not its soft underbelly, but its vital center.

As the physician heals himself, so does the country revivify after the debilitating bout with labor strife and economic depression: "During the next two years the country awoke from its torpor, feeling the blood tingle in its strong limbs once more, and rubbing its eyes in wonder at its own folly" (p. 331). America and Chicago had not, to be sure, solved their excruciating problems, but had merely shuffled them anew and were in the process of dealing a new hand for even bigger stakes. The point, as regards the ethical universe of *The Web of Life*, is that Dr. Howard Sommers is working and not stewing, doing his part to alleviate those dramatic problems by healing sundry American citizens with his art. His part is a modicum, certainly, but it is also taken in the novel to be the only sure thing an individual may do for his society, though no assurances are given that even a million such modicums will be enough for a place like Chicago. When Howard Sommers, inevitably, comes again to Louise Hitchcock, it is to find that she has learned as much about society as he. They marry, declining her father's proffered dowry; Sommers buys an unassuming neighborhood practice from a retiring physician; and they end the novel standing together firmly on the same middle social landscape. The lesson has taken, like an inoculation, and the implication is that neither the doctor nor his wife will require another.

Herrick's sense of place scarcely may be said to employ the traditional tricks of dialect, parochial mannerism, or setting. Instead he creates out of his Chicago materials what might be called a localized symbolic landscape. The fair and the Pullman strike were undeniably American events, as well as regional and local, and Herrick's accomplishment in his first Chicago novel is the investiture of these events and their scenes with palpable social meaning, meaning—translated into ethical dilemmas—for his characters to ponder and act upon. Inordinately fond as he is of such large concepts as will and life, Herrick is generally able to embody them credibly within his fiction. Ultimately, Howard Sommers's initiation is that of all modern Chicagoans, and the social significance in the novel is a significance refracted through his eyes. The local flavor, to the extent that it is there in *The Web of Life*, is dependent upon Herrick's symbolic use of events like the burning of the fair buildings and the desolation of the

Loop in a depression summer. And if Chicago continued to be the setting of many of Herrick's best novels, it was because Chicago was the very best place to study his version of the emerging American character.

The Common Lot (1904)

> The difference between the artist and the mind that works otherwise is that the artist must externalize his emotions, must objectify his moods, must express them in terms of human beings who are struggling with each other. And so in my case. My obsession with this phrase [*sic*] of spiritual abnegation and desire for forgiveness very soon expressed itself concretely in the figure of a young man, who having gone astray in the mazes of our modern high-keyed life and suffered some enormous shock, finds himself at springtime upon the bare earth, face to face with himself and his maker, with the power within him to rise once more and take on his shoulders the burden of living.... The repentant young man would be an architect.... And his temptation should be dishonest work.
>
> —Robert Herrick, "Myself"

These words constituted the germ for Herrick's *The Common Lot*, which appeared in the fall of 1904. As in the case of Henry Blake Fuller, Herrick was fascinated by the high dynamic of building going on in turn-of-the-century Chicago and saw the professional architect as a representative figure for the city and its society. But the pervasive influence in *The Common Lot* is Thorstein Veblen, and the theme of the novel may be found in Veblen's concept of the dichotomy between the instinct of workmanship and the predatory urge. Veblen had first advanced his idea of the instincts in *The Theory of the Leisure Class* (1899) and later elaborated upon it in *The Instinct of Workmanship and the State of the Industrial Arts* (1914).[11] In the latter essay Veblen described the features of this instinct: "The instinct of workmanship ... occupies the interest with practical expedients, ways and means, devices and contrivances of efficiency and economy, proficiency, creative work and technological mastery of facts. Much of the functional content of the instinct of workmanship is a proclivity for taking pains."[12] And in *The Theory of the Leisure Class* he indicated that when expediency and economy are stressed at the expense of the "creative work," the instinct of workmanship is sure to degenerate into the predatory emulation of wealth.[13] This happens to be almost paradigmatic for Herrick's story of his young architect, Jackson Hart, a man whose ambitious enthusiasm for building Chicago is corrupted by the race to make money rather than workmanlike edifices. And it is no exaggeration to say that Hart's buildings actually dominate the symbolic landscape of *The Common Lot* much as the Clifton towered over the Loop streets in *The Cliff-Dwellers*. It is the shoddy workmanship of Hart's Glenmore Hotel that makes it easy prey for a disastrous fire, and it is the derivative and aesthetically barren design of the Jackson Industrial Institute that lays bare the desiccation of the artisan's soul.

Herrick's irony in the novel is piercing: Jackson Hart's most damning moral failure is his association with the crooked contractor Graves and his corner-cutting, and therefore moneymaking, projects, including the ill-fated Glenmore; but Hart's most egregious artistic betrayal is the fiasco of the Industrial Institute—a building endowed by his uncle to glorify the instinct of workmanship in America! Hart's design is an *Ecole des Beaux Arts* imitation "straight from the Hotel de Ville."[14] The materials and actual building specifications are of the flimsiest and cheapest. In short, the monument to the instinct of workmanship turns out to be one of the most poorly crafted buildings in Chicago, and Jackson Hart is forced by circumstances to admit his moral bankruptcy, and then to begin the painful process of fully recognizing the social ethic of responsibility attached to being an architect—in America, in Chicago, in 1900.[15]

The initial instability in the novel is Jackson Hart's disappointment in his considerable expectations from a dead uncle's fortune. At the outset his notion of being an artist and an architect—the one inculcated both by his training and the social circles in which he moves—is to have sufficient means and leisure to create. He is worried lest his impressive Parisian *beaux arts* preparation be wasted, as it should be were he forced to go "into the ranks." But, without the inheritance, work he must; and Hart is soon caught up in the predatory competition for status: "His two years' experience in Chicago had taught him something about the fierceness of the struggle to exist in one of the professions, especially in a profession where there is an element of fine art. And his appetite to succeed, to be someone of note in this hurly-burly of Chicago, had grown very fast. For he had found himself less of a person in his native city than he had thought it possible over in Paris" (p. 29). The young architect errs badly, as do most of Herrick's protagonists, in formulating his personhood in social terms rather than individual. It is a mistake that precipitates many more as the novel unfolds.

Hart sees the same soul-deadening commercialism in architecture that had so sorely troubled Howard Sommers in medicine, but the designer in *The Common Lot* is attracted rather than repelled by the magnetism of social and economic competition. Was not the Chicago building climate the most favorable in the nation? Was not the need for housing greater than ever? And although Chicago boasted perhaps the most dynamic school of architecture in America—represented by the firm of Adler and Sullivan, with their disciple Frank Lloyd Wright, and by Burnham and Root, who had wrought the fair—the important thing was not what to build or how to build but simply to build and get a firmer grip on the main chance. Jackson Hart begins his career in the offices of the firm of Walker, Post, and Wright (the last-named member being a kind of rough-hewn, native American builder who gives Hart plenty of good advice which the Paris-trained young man scorns), but quickly decides to go it on his own. No sooner does he determine to set his own course than he hears a speech at his club on the rottenness of the contemporary professions: "The pity of it is that it ruins the professions. You can see it right here in Chicago. Who cares for fine professional work, if it don't bring in the stuff? Yes, look at our courts! look at our doctors! And look at our buildings. It's money every time. The professions have been commercialized" (pp. 54–55). This Mugwump discontent is put in perspective by a man named Pemberton—the same person who later uncovers Hart's shortcomings in the matter of the Jackon Industrial Institute. He speaks a recognizable Progressive line with hopeful fervor and sends a penetrating eye into the heart of the ambitious artchitect's motives:

> "Time has been when it meant something of honor for a man to be a member of one of the learned professions. Men were content to take part of their pay in honor and respect from the community. There's no denying that's all changed now. We measure everything by one yardstick, and that is money. So the able lawyer and the able doctor have joined the race with the mob for the dollars. But"—his eye seemed to rest on the young architect, who was listening attentively—"that state of affairs can't go on. When we shake down in this modern world of ours, and have got used to our wealth, and have made the right adjustments between capital and labor,—the professions, the learned professions, will be elevated once more. Men are so made that they want to respect something. And in the long run they will respect learning, ideas, and devotion to the public welfare" (p. 55).

The integrity of the professional was not surprisingly one of Robert Herrick's main moral preoccupations, and we can recognize in this passage more than an echo of Howard Sommers's concern in the earlier novel. In this case, however, the speaker is not himself the ethical agent but rather a sort of nemesis. And this is a sure sign that the lesson will be all the harder for Jackson Hart to learn.

Speeches like this one make it clear that Hart's desire to be a "money architect" is problematic in the novel, but there are potent naturalistic forces in Chicago that are difficult for him, indeed for anyone, to resist: "The noise, the smell, the reek of the city touched the man, folded him in, swayed him like a subtle opiate. The thirst of the terrible game of living, the desire of things, the brute love of triumph, filled his veins.... He, Jackson Hart, would show the world that he could fight for himself, could snatch the prize that every one was fighting for, the supreme prize of a man's life today—a little pot of gold" (pp. 63–64). Even Garland's larger-than-life Rose had not been able to shake off her fascination with "the terrible game of living" in Chicago, so endemic was it to the city. The baleful difference in the case of Hart is money—the insidious corrupter that Rose fortunately did not have to face.

Of course, the program demands that Hart realize how utterly wrong he is. Herrick's characterization of Jackson Hart is a careful one: he is cast as no mere business predator, no incarnate will to power, but rather as a Chicago man, different from the masses only by virtue of his artistic gifts and attendant sensibility, one who flows with his times without being conscious of the crucial ethical ramifications of his life's work. Hart's ambition to build quickly and profitably leads him first to opportunism, then to expediency, and finally to the verge of criminality. Yet the whole course of his decline he but dimly perceives, so adrift is he in the welter of tremendous forces that constitute his competitive life in the city. The reader, however, sees his degeneration all too clearly, heightened by the austere and uncompromising conscience of his wife, Helen, and made shockingly objective in the design model for the Industrial Institute.

Helen Hart is her husband's severest critic, and his behavior ultimately drives them to a separation. She had begun by loving Hart for the artist within him; and it was—like Alves Preston's love for Howard Sommers—an idealizing passion. Gradually, however, she discovers in him the drive antithetical to artistry. It is his "instinct for luxury" (p. 109)—an analogue of Veblen's idea of "pecuniary emulation"—which increasingly comes to qualify and eventually dominates his instinct for workmanship. Finally her dissatisfaction over Jackson's involvement with the unscrupulous contractor Graves and her learning of the cheating on the specification for the Institute cause her to leave. For Helen Hart is too conscientious to stay when her husband will not hear the truth about himself. Rather than expostulate with him she abruptly departs, a stern and insistent woman whose scrupulosity requires her rejection of his culpable behavior. She is one of Herrick's latter-day Puritans in the matter, but she is right.

Yet it is not Helen who sees deepest into Hart, but, ironically, his old boss Wright, who gazes upon the model for the Industrial Institute on display in the Art Institute and sees that the emptiness of the design reveals the emptiness in the designer:

> The design was splendid, in a sense—very large and imposing: an imperial flight of steps, a lofty dome which fastened the spectator's eyes, and two sweeping wings to support the central mass. Nevertheless, the architect had not escaped from his training; it was another of the Beaux Arts exercises that Wright used to "trim." Years hence the expert would assign it to its proper place in the imitative period of our arts, as surely as the literary expert has already placed the poet Longfellow. Though Hart had learned much in the past six years, it had been chiefly in the mechanics of his art: he was a cleverer architect, but a more wooden artist. For the years he had spent in the workshop of the great city had deadened his sense of beauty.... He had never had time to think, only to contrive, and facility had supplied the want of ideas. Thus he had forgotten beauty....
>
> So Wright read the dead soul beneath the ambitious design (pp. 261–62).

Herrick's irony becomes even more marvelously involuted when we recall that the Art Institute of Chicago, the building in which the display model proudly stood, was itself the product of the same derivative *Ecole des Beaux Arts* impulse—as had been the fair and dozens of other public buildings around the city, their commissions going to architects who specialized in imitations of French models which were themselves imitations of Italian Renaissance originals, while the more original, more "democratic and American" architects like Louis Sullivan struggled along in relative obscurity.[16]

The indirect reading of the artist in the art is worthy of Henry James, and Herrick develops the relation further by contrasting the grandiose plans for the institute with the actual construction, with the skimpings on foundations and grades of steel. Yet Hart can readily rationalize the result: "It was not a bad piece of work, after all, as Chicago building was done.... Even if Graves had cut the work in places ... the edifice would answer its purpose well enough, and the architect had no interest in the everlasting qualities of his structures. Nothing was built to stand for more than a generation in this city. Life moved too swiftly for that" (pp. 280–81). This sort of justification is as flimsy as Hart's buildings themselves, and starkly familiar to contemporary Chicagoans who, on the same specious logic, have seen such masterpieces as Sullivan's Stock Exchange Building demolished—but after two generations instead of one.

The betrayal of the instinct of workmanship in the Industrial Institute prepares us for the shock that will initiate Hart's regeneration: the appalling fire at the Glenmore Hotel. It turns out that many of the tenants of the hotel (not only built but jointly owned by Hart and Graves) die because the contractor had put no steel whatsoever in his "fireproof" building. Herrick brings the architect to the scene of the blaze in time to see the south wall of the hotel collapse, "shaking off the figures on the fire-escape as if they had been frozen flies. . . . He put his hands to his eyes and ran. He could hear the crowd in the street groaning with rage and pity" (pp. 320–21). As he had done with the burning of the abandoned White City in *The Web of Life*, Herrick uses the fire to represent not only death and destruction but also purification by flame of the impulses within his protagonist which had prompted shoddy artistry and the shriveling of the soul. Hart has much for which to atone. From the fire as well comes the relief of an admission of manifest guilt beyond rationalization, which in turn is the basis for spiritual rebirth. As Herrick had all along intended, Hart is rejuvenated by the inexhaustible healing power of the earth, after he finds himself alone in a field on the outskirts of the city, and realizes that for a long time "the earth had not spoken to him, alone, personally, out of her abundant wisdom, garnered through the limitless years" (p. 335). The land in—or very near—the city, with the same restorative force as the wilderness! For Hart that vacant lot becomes a place more important than all his buildings, the secret part of the urban landscape where he may lose his pitifully weak self and have born a new one annealed by the errors of the old. The most notable thing about Hart's mystical experience after the fire is that it prepares him for reentry into the vortex of Chicago. He will not withdraw but will seek his redemption among the very people he has wronged: his wife, those for whom he built, and the huge, amorphous Chicago public. Hart's self-awareness came by a transcendental agency, but Herrick deems it necessary that such self-knowledge be used toward the end of reestablishing a particular kind of ethical relationship with society—that of the Howellsian good citizen.

The trials, literal and figurative, to which Herrick subjects his protagonist after catastrophe and regeneration are arduous, designed to fit the ethical enormity of his past failings and to test the mettle Hart has so recently found within himself. Before the coroner's jury investigating the Glenmore fire he publicly admits his culpability in Graves' "skinning" on the hotel's specifications. And in those days, too, his infant son is stricken with illness and his life hangs in the balance. Would this, an infant's death, be part of the moral reparation? The dispensation in Herrick's ethical universe is finally more merciful than exacting: the infant is spared, and Jackson Hart escapes the full legal penalties for his weaknesses.

It is noteworthy that in this novel, as in the others, Herrick has no illusions about the ameliorative effect upon Chicago society of tragedies like the Glenmore Hotel fire and its public investigation:

> So the case against the men held to the Grand Jury for the hotel disaster was quietly dropped. The mayor put another man in Bloom's place as chief building inspector, and very soon things went merrily on in their old way. And that was the end of it all! The seventeen human beings who had lost their lives in the fire had not even pointed a moral by their agonizing death. For a few summer months the gaunt, smoke blackened pit of ruins in the boulevard served to remind the passersby of a grewsome tale. Then, by the beginning of the new year, in its place rose a splendid apartment building, faced with cut stone and trimmed with marble (pp. 396–97).

A new year, a new building. Perhaps Hart's earlier cynicism about nothing lasting or being remembered in Chicago was in part justified. For "morals" are not "pointed" for societies like America's, but only for such individuals as somehow are made capable of receiving them. If there is a possible salvation for American society, Herrick reiterates, it must be through socially saved individuals like Helen and Jackson Hart. For his part, Hart plunges, eyes fully open, into the ranks and accepts the common lot. He returns to the position he formerly despised with the firm of Wright and goes literally back to the drawing board. That wise old-schooler's view is the final judgment of Hart both as architect and man:

> As to Wright, who knows more of the man's real story than the others, he treats his old employee with a fine consideration and respect, realizing that this man is doing handsomely a thing that few men have the character to do at all. His admiration for Hart's work has grown, also, and he frankly admits that the younger man has a better talent for architecture than he himself ever possessed, as well as great cleverness and ingenuity, so necessary in an art which is intimately allied with mechanics. For it is true that after sluggish years there has revived within Hart the creative impulse, that spirit

of the artist, inherent to some extent in all men, which makes the work of their hands an engrossing joy. The plans of a group of buildings, which the firm have undertaken for a university in a far Western state, have been entrusted very largely to Hart. As they grow from month to month in the voluminous sheets of drawings, they are becoming the pride of the office, and Wright generously allots the praise for their beauty where it largely belongs (p. 420).

This fine passage is about the revitalization of the instinct of workmanship, a revitalization of the deepest morality of the "creative impulse ... inherent to some extent in all men" made possible by a commitment to decent dealing on the level of the social ethic. Hart is not only given another chance with Wright's firm: he is also given another (symbolic) chance to be the artisan. Where he had failed in the design and construction of the Jackson Industrial Institute, he admirably succeeds in the master plan for a new "far Western" university. These buildings-to-be are praised by Wright for their "beauty," a word which we may imagine the master architect uses sparingly, and which he had not used at all as he had sadly pondered the plans for the institute. In the end it is Helen who convinces her husband to resume his old position: "We are all trying to get out of the ranks, to leave the common work to be done by others, to be leaders. We think it a disgrace to stay in the ranks, to work for the work's sake, to bear the common lot, which is to live humbly and labor!" (p. 402). Her earnest words recall the more famous ones of William Dean Howells in *Criticism and Fiction*, words already seen in these pages, about "struggling to be distinguished from the mass, and to be set apart in the select circles and upper classes," about the essential American vulgarity of ignoring "the worth of the vulgar" and thinking the superfine better. In *The Common Lot* Robert Herrick wrote one of the American novels which came closest to fulfilling Howells's program for American realism. For both men the kind of society they could affirm was fast receding from possibility in fact—in Chicago and in America at large—but they held fast to their insistence in fiction that if enough good men did something it still might be.

The Memoirs of an American Citizen (1905)

> You, gentlemen, are the revolutionists! You rebel against
> the effects of social conditions which have tossed you, by the
> fair hand of fortune, into a magnificent paradise. Without
> enquiring, you imagine that no one else has a right in that

place. You insist that you are the chosen ones, the sole
proprietors. The forces that tossed you into the paradise, the
industrial forces, are still at work. They are growing more
active and intense from day to day. Their tendency is to
elevate all mankind to the same level, to have all humanity
share in the paradise you now monopolize. You, in your
blindness, think you can stop the tidal wave of civilization.

—August Spies

These words were spoken by Spies at his trial for conspiracy to commit murder—part of the infamous anarchists' trial which followed the so-called Haymarket Riot of 4 May 1886. August Spies was one of the four men who remained true to their ideology to the last: he was hanged on 11 November 1887, and this was the "civic murder" which was so horrifying to William Dean Howells and other liberally minded Americans across the land.[17] Beyond the obvious and deplorable injustice done to the anarchists, beyond even the shocking abrogation of First-Amendment freedoms sanctioned by a befuddled and anxious American society, is the critical power of the thought of men like Spies and his fellow radical Albert Parsons. Spies's address at his trial can hardly be a legal defense. It is more in the mode of a Socratic apology, designed to convince nobody but posterity, but certain through its moral force to do just that. The word *paradise* occurs three times in the brief passage. Industrialization, according to Spies, had created an urban paradise of wealth and leisure and happiness. Yet the process was now being interpreted feudally rather than democratically by the managers, as if some very special and providential ticket were needed to enter the industrial paradise. The element missing from this now-familiar dialectic between workers and managers is the great American middle class, and yet from that class alone was to come the lasting social critique of "paradise." The plutocrats were in the garden and loving it; the lowly workers saw its shining portico and struggled for admission. The poles of American society appeared to affirm the new urban utopia, and only from the middle came any demurral.[18]

Robert Herrick had not been around the Chicago scene in 1886. In that year he was still safely cloistered at Harvard and would not think of leaving the order for quite a while. Still, for his most ambitious Chicago novel he looked back to the time of the great strike at International Harvester (McCormick Reaper Works) and even before, to the actual genesis of labor difficulties in the western city. Most everything within his fiction hitherto he had seen: indeed the closeness with events in Chicago had made them disturbingly tangible. Now, however, he was forced to imagine, almost twenty years after the facts, what Haymarket and its aftermath had been like. He had in mind a first-person novel, a "fictional autobiography" in which a self-made plutocrat would tell his own story to a nation hungry for such romance—the romance of business, or "the romance of fact," as Henry James called it.[19] It would tell the business-man's side of things. It would be affirmative, justificatory, inspirational, a kind of plainspoken, typically American *Apologia pro Vita Sua.* The result was *The Memoirs of an American Citizen* (1905), and the only difference between the story told by E. V. "Van" Harrington, meat-packing king, and the story the reader digests is the fact that the businessman's apology is totally unacceptable on a moral level. Herrick, in a masterwork of satire, has cynically and with devastating irony undercut the stereotype of the American success story at every point. The more Van Harrington prides himself on his depredations in the Chicago marketplace, the more we (with Herrick) demur over his uncritical acceptance of the operating methods of finance capitalism. Ironic as he is, though, Harrington is a superb portrait. He comes alive as a kind of capitalistic everyman, just another of the numberless "American citizens" running so doggedly after the main chance, never looking up to see where they are. Van Harrington is convinced that the end—in this case a romantic landscape quite similar to Spies's paradise—easily justifies the means of getting there. Herrick is equally convinced that both end and means are disastrous: there is no paradise in Chicago and pursuit of a delusion is demoralizing and human-ly hurtful. And since Herrick is doing the talking in Harrington's "memoirs" we must inevitably see things his way.

Van Harrington's final state is perhaps the place to begin. In a passage near the end of the novel the by-now hugely successful Harrington pauses in the midst of "his Chicago" to take stock of his life:

> Traffic, business, industry,—the work of the world was going forward. A huge lumber boat blocked the river at the bridge, and while the tugs pushed it slowly through the draw, I stood and gazed at the busy tracks in the railroad yards below me, at the line of warehouses along the river. I, too, was a part of this. The thought of my brain, the labor of my body, the will within me, had gone to the making of this world. There were my plants, my car line, my railroads, my elevators, my lands—all good tools in the infinite work of the world. Conceived for good or for ill, brought into being by fraud or daring,—what man could judge *their* worth? There they were, a part of God's great world. They were done; and mine was the hand. Let another, more perfect, turn them to a larger use;

nevertheless, on my labor, on me, he must build.

Involuntarily, my eyes rose from the ground and looked straight before me, to the vista of time. Surely there was another scale, a grander one, and by this I should not be found wholly wanting![20]

Harrington is made to speak in the simplistic logic and with the self-inflating rhetoric of the social Darwinist: he is awed in the presence of a vast physical tranformation and feels that perforce he must have had much to do with it. But the logical leap from the observation "there they were" to the assertion "mine was the hand" is a dubious one to all save Harrington himself. It is clear that Herrick does not expect his anti-hero to show any exquisite moral sense, but he does emphasize the irony of Harrington's arrogant and facile belief that he is the prime mover behind Chicago's physical explosion. In a manner similar to Dreiser's Frank Cowperwood (in *The Titan*), Harrington in his rude way attempts a "Chicago apotheosis" of himself. When he thinks of his "plants and warehouses," he mellows; when his trampling upon society is brought to mind, he dismisses such thoughts as "sentimental reflection" (p. 343). When packing houses are raised up in the name of "another scale, a grander one," then means qua means are inconsiderable, obscured in the long shadow of the glorious end. The final irony in *Memoirs* is that Harrington is so consumed by the money-madness of Chicago that he genuinely considers himself, in spite of the naturalistic evidence to the contrary, the heroic, neofeudal lord of all he surveys. It is the logical and deliciously ironical outcome of the American self-made model: he has never been beaten, so the game itself is rightfully his. Harrington *is* Chicago, for his "was the hand."

At the beginning of *Memoirs* we had seen Van Harrington learning the system even before he left the farm:

While I was sweating on that farm I saw the folly of running against common notions about property. I came to the conclusion that if I wanted what my neighbor considered to be his, I must get the law to do the business for me. For the first time it dawned on me how wonderful is that system which shuts up one man in jail for taking a few dollars worth of truck that doesn't belong to him, and honors the man who steals his millions—if he robs in the legal way! (pp. 20–21).

Ah, yes, white-collar crime—and Harrington is about ready to change shirts! This is the right outlook for the modern business predators, but it does not accord with the romanticizing of Harrington's final apology several hundred pages and twenty-five years later. It is the need on Harrington's part to find a metaphysical significance in what is really pure exploitation that opens the ironic distance between the businessman and the reader. If Harrington were merely a clever LaSalle Street or Packingtown picaro we should hardly be offended by his wheeling and dealing, for it would then be seen as the comic manifestation of an activity which has come in our own day to be revealingly known as "making it." But Harrington must have meaning, and what rankles is his self-representation as his ego would have him painted: as a kind of medieval donor before his castle, only with greater presumption, since he is not merely placing himself in the sanctified company of this or that saint but is looking to be canonized. Early on, the hustling newcomer to the city is fond of speaking of the "golden road" on which he is starting to travel, and in those scrambling years he burns the midnight oil reading Darwin, Spencer, and Lecky, and "a lot more hard nuts" (p. 63) to find a rationale for what he is learning to do from watching the business adepts around him. Social Darwinism is the pseudoscience of the age in Chicago (as in America), and its tenets give him precisely the ideology he needs to push relentlessly upward: "Whatever was there in Chicago in 1877 to live for but Success?" (p. 52).

The midpoint—both symbolic and actual—in Harrington's business ascent comes about ten years after his discovery of what success in Chicago is. The fierce and cruel decade of labor strife is about to begin with the affair at Haymarket, and, as he had done with the fair and the Pullman strike in *The Web of Life*, Herrick puts his protagonist smack in the middle of the drama of Chicago's social history as it is playing out. Harrington is thrust into the center of the stage by being selected for the jury which is to hear the case against the anarchists. It is a jury Harrington knows to be "safe," guaranteed to return the proper verdict, no matter what the evidence, a jury to which "no working man need apply; his class was suspect" (p. 88). Herrick shows characteristic historical accuracy in the use of details: the jury was safe, the evidence that the defendants were in any way associated with the unknown bomb-thrower nonexistent, the verdict a foregone conclusion based on a hysteria of fear and hate.[21] Yet the "American citizen" accepts without question the course of events: it is "all a parcel of lies," the "one motive" is fear, but still one's "duty to society" must be performed. For Van Harrington the entire matter is reduced to a "struggle between sensible folks who went about their business and tried to get all there was in it . . . and some scum from Europe" (p. 92). The rather laborious irony here is that the

American citizen, by his own admission, is caught up in the most important event of the decade in Chicago (and it is easy for us to see today how formative the Haymarket events were of subsequent American thought and behavior), but is unable to exercise a single critical or individual judgment about either the trial itself or his culpable role in it.

He is lucky enough to find himself on the "right side" of the issue, and his relief is enough to dispel any lingering doubts he might have had about his own conduct: "It was comfortable to be of the strong. The world is for the strong, I said to myself as I left the court, and I am one of them!" (p. 97). This is the most venal form of the might makes right ethic. Harrington's kind of strength can never admit the moral strength of the anarchists, who faced death squarely for their principles. They had simply, in Harrington's jargon, "lost their nerve." The memorial of the incident, when it would be later erected over by the Chicago River, was not for the anarchists but for the seven policemen killed in the melee. And when another wave of radicalism hit the city in the late 1960s, a twenty-four-hour guard was established to protect the memory of police civic sacrifice from defacement by "some scum" from the colleges or ghettoes. Eventually, the statue was moved away from the actual place of the Haymarket events, and few who pass by the scene today realize the significance of the ground on which they walk. One can imagine Van Harrington subscribing to the fund for the building of such a monument, and in the symbolic act one can sense the full force of Robert Herrick's belief, stated earlier, that Chicago was built by the wrong people for the wrong reasons. To most of those who passed the monument it was just another statue, one among anonymous hundreds of public tokens throughout the city. To some other few it was a monument to infamy and injustice. And to still others it represented a proud reminder that Chicago—their tough Chicago—had had the nerve to show "them" what America was all about.

Half a dozen years after Haymarket came the exposition, and of course Van Harrington has got to take it in. By 1893 he is accelerating toward the kingship of Chicago's enormous meat-packing industry, he is becoming supremely confident of his exalted place in Chicago society, and the fair provides a nice opportunity to rhapsodize on his favorite theme, the triumph of the business will:

> The long lines of white buildings were ablaze with countless lights; the music from the bands scattered over the grounds floated softly out upon the water; all else was silent and dark. In that lovely hour,

soft and gentle as was ever a summer night, the toil and trouble of men, the fear that was gripping men's hearts in the market, fell away from me, and in its place came Faith. The people who could dream this vision and make it real, those people from all parts of the land who thronged here day after day—their sturdy wills and strong hearts would rise above failure, would press on to greater victories than this triumph of beauty—victories greater than the world had yet witnessed! (p. 192).

If Van Harrington is articulating the faith of a Walt Whitman, Herrick deftly turns it into only a mocking echo of the old optimism, for it is a faith grounded not on American democracy but on the stock market. And, to be sure, is not after all real; it is stucco and wood and all frosted rococo gingerbread, not designed to endure more than the year of its planned tenure. Harrington's affirmations are not intended to convince, for Herrick no longer believes in them himself: just as the stock market is no serious epitome for America's social problems or progress, so is the fair (after more than a decade's reflection on Herrick's part) only a sham ceremony in the earthly manifestation of ideals. Dazzled by his success, the American citizen can still espouse a version of the outmoded idealism, though it is clear he should take his eyes from the zenith long enough to have a look at the muck beneath him on the nadir. All Harrington's connivings, bribings, preemptions are executed in the name of some vague and metaphysical "greatest good," while the immediate and imperative social needs of the greatest number are denied when they are recognized at all.

The acute solipsism of the American business tycoon is by now a familiarly diagnosed part of the pathology of the type, but Herrick deserves credit for giving us an interesting and an early case study. Van Harrington at his pinnacle is denounced from the pulpit: all these social gospel preachers are "silk-stockings" (for contemporary translation read "effete snobs"). He is excoriated by the press: the newspapers are nothing but political house organs. He alienates his wife and his brother and sister-in-law: none of them understands him or his high purpose. The self is all that may be known. Harrington claims to know himself. He pleases himself. And he creates the industrial landscape around him in his own dreary image.

This world, which he does not feel is incommensurate with the White City, is a new feudal order, a necessary and desirable outcome of the march of finance capitalism and technology, and as such it is no longer subject to the democratic social contract—"You, gentlemen, are the revolutionists!" Democracy, Harrington says, "proved itself inadequate in a short century.... But we men who did the work of the world, who developed the country, who were the life and force of the times, could not be held back by the swaddling clothes of any political or moral theory" (pp. 246–47). From their fiefdoms in the Chicago industrial districts, from the dark towers of LaSalle Street, these princes with their legal Merlins unleash the fury of their stock-corners, turn back the strike-sieges of the unions which represent the commons. And when Harrington is sent to the United States Senate, he goes as a guardian of his own and the other meat-packers' interests—there is no question of any national perspective, no implication of any constituency beyond the Loop and Packingtown.

Herrick slips one parting irony into *Memoirs:* Harrington, having bought his Senate seat, is forced to realize that he cannot buy a place on the United States Supreme Court for his lifelong friend and legal counsel, Jaffrey Slocum. Slocum had for years done Harrington's dirty work in the courts, had been that manipulator of the law Harrington knew he would need even before he left Indiana. No corporation lawyer who had muddied his hands to the extent Slocum had been forced to could hope to sit on the "Supreme Bench." For here at least was one American institution that Herrick regarded as yet beyond purchase. It is consistent with Harrington's entire career that the one check society is able to make on him ultimately hurts not the financier but his trusted lieutenant.

After *The Memoirs of an American Citizen*, Robert Herrick altered his novelistic perspective toward Chicago and urban society in general. When he wrote subsequently about the problems of predatory capitalism, as he did in *A Life for a Life* (1910), it was in terms of an apocalyptic allegory of social disintegration; when he once again treated the recurrent theme of an individual's relationship to social institutions, it was from the inner psychological point of view, as in his examination of marriage in *Together* (1908). Thus the Chicago trio of *The Web of Life*, *The Common Lot*, and *Memoirs* stands today as Herrick's collective contribution to the phase of American fiction grounded in the drama of the average American's attempts to accommodate himself to the bewildering changes in the urban-industrial society—trying to find the delicate ethical balance between getting on and preempting.

In his use of Chicago materials Herrick was not a local-colorist. He understood regional subject matter and technique but was striving to create the sort of richly complex ethical universe he saw and admired in the work of Howells and Henry James. To this end local color for its own sake would have been an impediment. He chose as a more effective means the localized symbolic landscape: the anarchist riot and trial, the Pullman strike and its aftermath, and, most symbolically suggestive of all, the World's Columbian Exposition. Herrick's patient dedication to Howells's program for American realism, adapted to fit the Chicago novelist's preoccupation with the organic social structure of his adopted city, resulted in three novels that are among the best things he ever wrote. And they are the best midwestern expressions of the Progressive impulse in American fiction.

NOTES—CHAPTER V

1. Adapted from my essay, "Robert Herrick: A Chicago Trio," *Old Northwest*, 1 (Mar. 1975), 63–84, and used by permission.
2. Robert Herrick, *The Gospel of Freedom* (New York: Macmillan Co., 1898), p. 101.
3. Blake Nevius, *Robert Herrick: The Development of a Novelist* (Berkeley: University of California Press, 1962), pp. 53–55.
4. Nevius, *Robert Herrick*, p. 56.
5. Robert Herrick, *A Life for a Life* (New York: Macmillan Co., 1910), pp. 427–28.
6. The company town of Pullman, Illinois, was the scene for one of the bitterest of the early wars between unionizing labor and entrenching management. George M. Pullman was an autocrat who thought himself progressive for having built (on the far South Side of the city) a rather pleasant place for his men to live and work, but in fact Pullman, Illinois, was a shrewdly conceived means of keeping the money in the family. To live in the company houses a worker was forced to sign a lease promising, in addition to the usual things, never to enter his "castle" with muddy feet and not to drive a picture nail into the wall without written permission from a superintendent. Herrick is accurate on the question of the first layoffs going to workers who lived outside the community (see Stanley Buder's *Pullman* and Almont Lindsey's *The Pullman Strike*).
7. Robert Herrick, *The Web of Life* (New York: Macmillan Co., 1900), pp. 33–34. Subsequent references are contained within the body of the essay.
8. I am not using the term in its strictest political sense (i.e., affiliation with "Mugwump" third-party politics), but rather as Richard Hofstadter has so well described it: "The newly rich, the grandiosely or corruptly rich, the masters of great corporations, were bypassing the men of the Mugwump type—the old gentry, the merchants of long standing ... the established professional men.... In their personal careers, as in their community activities, they found themselves checked.... They were less important, and they knew it" (*The Age of Reform* [New York: Random House Vintage Books, 1960], p. 137).

9. Disregarding the authority of Illinois governor John Altgeld, President Grover Cleveland ordered federal troops into Chicago from Ft. Sheridan on 3 July 1894 (see Almont Lindsey, *The Pullman Strike,* for a full analysis of the federal intervention).

10. Readers might be interested in comparing Herrick's use of the Pullman strike with another fictional treatment of the same events: Octave Thanet [Mary Alice French], *The Man of the Hour* (1905). Her protagonist, Johnny-Ivan Winslow, is among the leaders of the Pullman strike, and some of the descriptions of the confrontations and the severe winter of 1894-95 are very graphic indeed. However, Thanet's Winslow, far from learning any sort of progressive social lesson from his labor involvement, ends up back home in Iowa, managing a factory (the inheritance from "his own") and busting its fledgling union.

11. Veblen is not mentioned in Blake Nevius's biography of Herrick, even though all three of the novels under consideration here were written while Veblen and Herrick were both at the University of Chicago and while Veblen's devastating *Theory of the Leisure Class* was spreading its provocative social message among the intellectuals of America. But there may well have been a more or less direct influence. Because Herrick was so thoroughly a social novelist, he would surely have been aware of Veblen's critical analyses of American institutions, manners, and mores. The notion of the instinct of workmanship and its betrayal by a society ruled by canons of predatory emulation and conspicuous consumption would seem to be ready-made for embodiment in the kinds of human dramas Herrick favored: those of man's natural proclivities denied or perverted by unhealthy social forces, then reclaimed in the moral regeneration of the principals. Beyond the question of whether they knew each other personally lies the fact of their mounting similarly conceived and similarly incisive critiques of American society—and doing so from the same place at roughly the same time.

12. Thorstein Veblen, *The Instinct of Workmanship and the State of the Industrial Arts* (New York: Augustus M. Kelley, 1964), p. 33.

13. Thorstein Veblen, *The Theory of the Leisure Class* (New York: Random House Modern Library, 1931), p. 93.

14. Robert Herrick, *The Common Lot* (New York: Macmillan Co., 1904), p. 260. Subsequent references are contained within the body of the essay.

15. In what strikes me as a superb continuation of the Veblen tradition of social analysis, as applied to architecture, James Ackerman has recently written an essay treating the moral dimension in American architecture ("Transactions in Architectural Design," *Critical Inquiry,* 1 [Dec. 1974], 229–43). Ackerman asserts that "the architect has a wide latitude of choice, particularly in our time, when the institutions that build are too insecure and uncertain about the future to define what they want their buildings to do or to express. Left without guidance, the architect is forced to choose [how to proceed].... This choice is moral ... it involves the option of acting on a sense of responsibility to society with the consequent risks incurred by departing from a pragmatic position of self-interests" (pp. 240–41). Ackerman ends with the reaffirmation of an idea that certainly was central to the architectural creed of

Louis Sullivan and others of the Chicago school: the architect is responsible "toward the whole company of those affected by his invention" (p. 243).

16. Louis Sullivan got precisely one commission for the fair: the Transportation Building. But its architectural simplicity and monolithic power were in sharp distinction to the other structures. To one leafing through a portfolio of photographs of the exposition today, the astounding Golden Door to the building comes as a revelation of native American authority amid the vast white imitation. Ironically, the design won him a medal from the *Societe des Arts Decoratifs*. Sullivan's evaluation of the exposition is summed up in his famous statement that "the damage wrought by the World's Fair will last for half a century from its date, if not longer" (quoted in Condit, *Chicago School of Architecture*, p. 136).

17. Concerning the trial and its outcome Howells wrote his sister, "Annie, it's all been an atrocious piece of frenzy and cruelty, for which we must stand ashamed before history" (*Life in Letters of William Dean Howells* [Garden City, N.Y.: Doubleday, Doran and Co., 1928], I, 404).

18. That the beleaguered wage slave was afflicted with a romantic view of the industrial paradise may seem strange, but so long as he thought he could rise through the ranks, could take the journey to it, he was positively motivated. See the saga of Jurgis Rudkus (*The Jungle*) below in Ch. VI.

19. In Henry James, *American Letters* (1898).

20. Robert Herrick, *The Memoirs of an American Citizen* (New York: Macmillan Co., 1905), p. 346. Subsequent references are contained within the body of the essay.

21. See Albert Fried, ed., *Socialism in America* (New York: Doubleday, Anchor, 1970), pp. 188–90; and Chester McArthur Destler, *American Radicalism, 1865–1901* (Chicago: Quadrangle, 1966), pp. 101–3. Readers may also want to look at Frank Harris's *The Bomb* (1908), a novel which fictionalizes the Haymarket events in great detail.

CHAPTER VI

The City of Excess and Beyond

> Of my city the worst that men will ever say is this:
> You took little children away from the sun and the dew,
> And the glimmers that played in the grass under the great sky,
> And the reckless rain; you put them between walls
> To work, broken and smothered, for bread and wages,
> To eat dust in their throats and die empty-hearted
> For a little handful of pay on a few Saturday nights
>
> —Carl Sandburg, "They Will Say"

The Vortex and the Jungle

In the voice of Carl Sandburg—the archetypal Chicago voice of the twentieth century—irony barely holds back the freshets of sentimentality that are forever on the verge of breaking through. And behind the irony lies the full naturalistic horror of the urban jungle, the American heart of darkness in Chicago. The first decade and a half of the twentieth century, climaxing in the publication of Sandburg's *Chicago Poems* in 1916, completed for Chicago what the fair and the 1890s had so energetically begun: a coherent image of the city emerged in the American national consciousness. Once and for all Chicago lost its regional insularity. Yet neither this process of emergence nor the nature of Chicago's national image were such as would please the typical middle-class citizens of the city, principally because Chicago came to be depicted more and more as the anti-utopia of industrialization rather than the burgher's paradise they tried to keep in mind as the city exploded with growth. Certainly Chicago had its vocal national boosters, writers and public figures who offered the nation at large a positive view of their city. Syndicated columnists like Peter Finley Dunne ("Mr. Dooley") and George Ade reached America both through their newspaper columns and the books in which these rosy vignettes of local color and human nature were later collected. They stressed the humorous aspects of countless individuals on the make in a city loaded with juicy opportunity. Why not Horatio Alger? The paradigm had worked for them, for their friends, for lots of folks who had followed sound and smoke and tower from the country to the city: hence the inviolable generality—pull hard and long on those bootstraps and you would get there. This was all a part of the American gospel of success, familiar and, one would think, acceptable to the millions across the land who listened to the news from Chicago. Surprisingly, however, the gospel failed to take. For where Chicago is concerned we have come to believe and say the worst about the city, a tendency which shows no sign of being eradicated from the national mythology.

To help us see that this is so, ask the question, "What is the most notorious novel ever written about Chicago?" Upton Sinclair's *The Jungle* (1905). There really aren't any other serious contenders. This is the book read by people who otherwise have no sense of Chicago, past or present; it is the book whose dire message has been assimilated by three generations of schoolchildren in Illinois, to be sure, but also in California and New York. *The Jungle* is frequently credited with bringing about more social reform that all the "new broom" political movements put together and for molding popular opinion more effectively than any educational campaign ever devised. But in the story of the social impact of *The Jungle* two important facts are often overlooked: Upton Sinclair intended the book to make a persuasive case for American socialism, and, when no socialist political mandate was forthcoming, he regarded his exposé of the Chicago meat-packing industry as a failure. "I aimed at the public's heart," he lamented, "and by accident I hit it in the stomach."[1] People for a time stopped eating the "embalmed beef" of Packingtown, but hardly rose up spontaneously to establish the socialist commonwealth. Sinclair had wanted socialism but got only the Pure Food and Drug Act—a guarantee not that the workers of Chicago and America would no longer be exploited but that middle-America's meat would be more wholesome. *The Jungle* a failure? Perhaps to Upton Sinclair, the idealist. But to the Illinoisans who have inherited its uncompromising tradition of social criticism the novel remains crucial.

The Jungle was one of the last American novels to attempt on a panoramic scale a synthesis and a reconciliation of the grandiose paradoxes inherent in our democracy. Sinclair saw and lived through the horrendous deprivations and degradations of the workingman in Chicago's stockyards and packing plants and tried in his fiction to be as true to that physical reality as he could. That he envisioned the final solution to America's social ills as a political transvaluation is a reflection of his commitment to socialism. Yet his depiction of raw, unrelieved, and unrelenting human waste and agony among the immigrants "back of the yards" reads today as a sensitive humanitarian's last-ditch attempt, in the name of all Americans, to make sense out of the country's abysmal class situation. The dedication of *The Jungle* was "to the Workingmen of America,"[2] and the book's title represented, in the memorable words of Walter Rideout, "a feat of imaginative compression, for the world in which the Lithuanian immigrant Jurgis [Rudkus] and his family find themselves is an Africa of unintelligibility, of suffering and terror, where the strong beasts devour the weak, who are dignified, if at all, only by their agony."[3] The betrayal of democracy, the heinous hypocrisies of the melting pot and the progressive factory system—these Sinclair had seen for himself in Chicago and these he passionately indicted as the socially destructive evils they were. But it was for the plight of the individual caught in the unholy web of urban circumstance that he reserved his most chilling naturalism. *The Jungle* opens with a marvelous local-color description of the wedding celebration of Jurgis Rudkus and his beloved Ona. The initial pages are brimming with the folklife of the immigrants, which is still hearty and has not yet begun withering at the roots from transplantation. It is certainly no exaggeration to say that this is the last pleasant representation for three hundred pages. The rest of the novel— at least as far as the paean to socialism at the end—is one continuous onslaught of inhuman industrial horror.

Readers today can hardly wonder that Sinclair "hit the public in the stomach." *The Jungle* screams at us to look and be appalled. Yet in a way the sustained scream arises from narrative silence. The matter-of-fact tone in such passages as the following is typical of Sinclair's technique throughout the novel: let the graphic truth induce pity and fear in the hearts of the readers.

> There was no heat upon the killing beds; the men might exactly as well have worked out of doors all winter. For that matter, there was very little heat anywhere in the building.... On the killing beds you were apt to be covered with blood, and it would freeze solid; if you leaned against a pillar, you would freeze to that, and if you put your hand upon the blade of your knife, you would run a chance of leaving your skin on it. The men would tie up their feet in newspapers and old sacks, and these would be soaked in blood and frozen, and then soaked again, and so on, until by nighttime a man

would be walking on great lumps the size of the feet of an elephant. Now and then, when the bosses were not looking, you would see them plunging their feet and ankles into the steaming hot carcass of the steer, or darting across the room to the hot-water jets. The cruelest thing of all was that nearly all of them—all of those who used knives—were unable to wear gloves, and their arms would be white with frost and their hands would grow numb, and then of course there would be accidents. Also the air would be full of steam, from the hot water and the hot blood, so that you could not see five feet before you; and then, with men rushing about at the speed they kept up on the killing beds, and all with butcher knives, like razors, in their hands—well, it was to be counted as a wonder that there were not more men slaughtered than cattle (pp. 83–84).

In this long extract there is but one word which could be termed judgmental on the author's part, "cruelest." The rest is an objective relation: this is the way things are, and America's working class, in its infinite malleability, adapts and endures. The passage concludes with an irony—akin to Sandburg's "the worst that men will say" but cruder—that universalizes the horror and leaves us muttering, "there but for the grace...."

The overall picture of Packingtown, city of Chicago, is one of a seething cauldron of class-hatred, race-hatred, and unspeakable human waste. There is the poor foolish clerk in the front office who labors in utter servitude for a few dollars a week, but will not condescend to speak to a "mere laborer"; then there are the cruel Irish bosses, politically so well connected, who literally spit on the "new" immigrants from Eastern and Southern Europe; and, of course, everybody reviles the black scabs brought up from the South by the boxcar load to break a strike in the yards and plants. To teach *The Jungle* in a literature class, particularly to so-called ethnic adults in urban continuing education classes, is to see that something can be learned from our history: race and class prejudices are one and the same aberration.[4] The Poles and Lithuanians who today so unquestioningly accept the inherited prejudice against blacks are apt to take a second look when confronted with the drama of their own degradation at the hands of the already established Irish around the turn of the century. The dissolution of the Rudkus family is an American object lesson of the first order. By novel's end the tightly knit family unit that had come to America only a few years before is decimated, several of its members dead and the others dispersed to fend for themselves in Packingtown's tenderloin. When Jurgis Rudkus finally learns the whereabouts of his cousin, Marija, he seeks her out and finds her in a whorehouse. She has lost any vestige of the old-country ways that would cause mortification at such a meeting, and she proceeds nonchalantly to rehearse for Jurgis the recent family history:

> "How long have you been living here?" he asked.
> "Nearly a year," she answered.
> "Why did you come?"
> "I had to live," she said; "and I couldn't see the children starve."
> He paused for a moment, watching her. "You were out of work?" he asked, finally.
> "I got sick," she replied, "and after that I had no money. And then Stanislovas died—"
> "Stanislovas dead!"
> "Yes," said Marija, "I forgot. You didn't know about it."
> "How did he die?"
> "Rats killed him," she answered.
> Jurgis gave a gasp. "*Rats* killed him!"
> "Yes," said the other; she was bending over, lacing her shoes as she spoke. "He was working in an oil factory—at least he was hired by the men to get their beer. He used to carry cans on a long pole; and he'd drink a little out of each one, and one day he drank too much, and fell asleep in a corner, and got locked up in the place all night. When they found him the rats had killed and eaten him nearly all up" (p. 286).

This is not to be confused with the exquisite horror of an Edgar Allan Poe tale: Stanislovas is a boy and his end is an obscenity. In similar fashion the imported Lithuanian folk culture quickly decays and dies. Tamozius, the violinist for the community's celebrations and feasts, Tamozius, the freest spirit among them and the symbol of the beauty and magic of the European folk heritage—well, Tamozius must work too in America, for the violin is a joy and an avocation: first he loses a finger in his packing-house job, then contracts blood poisoning and ruins his hand, and finally just drops out of sight, into the urban vortex, unlamented and even unmissed. *The Jungle* relentlessly shows everything vital brought to America by the Europeans ultimately destroyed in the disastrous process of their Americanization. Sinclair's point is that the price of "making it"[5] in America is often too high and that the exacting of the price does not itself guarantee success. And when the ephemeral solace of success is denied to those who have been used up in its pursuit, what remains? For Upton Sinclair there was always the promise of America socialism somewhere down the road, but few of the downtrodden could muster Sinclair's consoling idealist's dreams. They were forced to take the longer, rougher road of trade unionism, which in a protracted series of battles with capital eventually banished forever the worst excesses of Packingtown. This twentieth-century crusade, one of the great social dramas in American history, owes at least a small part of its achievement to that solid belt to the American public's midsection administered by a sensational novel which insisted that even the bewildered immigrant from God knows where was, or ought to be, a citizen of the republic— and not an insignificant lump of raw material for America's voracious industrial monster.

Over the years Sinclair's image of the jungle has become one of our definitive urban metaphors, associated not only with Chicago but with American cities generally. Yet, as we have seen, the jungle was but one among a group of potent figures—the cliff-dwellers, the procession, the web of life—and one final example remains to be discussed: Frank Norris's *The Pit* (1903). A few miles north of Packingtown by trolley but light years away in social sensibility, "the Pit" was the wheat-futures trading area at the Chicago Board of Trade—in the 1890s the frenetic center of Chicago's financial empire on LaSalle Street.[6] As one can still see today, the Pit was literally just that: the agents of fortune descended into its mouth to transact the business of futures trading, on which the price of the world's bread depended, then climbed out again to catch a furtive glimpse of the Big Board above them—in hopes of learning what their bargains with the impersonal forces of economics had wrought. And in this very act of bartering with unseen presences we catch the metaphorical essence of Norris's "Pit." It is the timeless opening to perdition, forever gaping and yawning and drawing even the strongest wills down into its final evil. Frank Norris was among the first American writers to see the objective power of the economics of finance capitalism as an immoral force, and the Faustian bargain of a talented and nervy speculator with the whirlwind of the Pit became the subject of the last novel the young writer completed before his untimely death in 1902.

Frank Norris was a turn-of-the-century romantic without a hero. He loved the greatness of nature and tended to write and speak of it with upper-case emphasis: Nature was almighty and the Wheat was the principal manifestation of her power in America. Sown and reaped by farmers, processed, baked, and distributed by middlemen, consumed around the world as the staff of life—yet with a life of its own, the wheat was immeasurably greater than any one man, greater even than the set of institutions mankind designed to control it. *The Pit* was the second novel in Norris's projected trilogy, "The Epic of Wheat." The first novel had been called *The Octopus* (1901) and had centered around the growing of the wheat in California's San Joaquin Valley. *The Pit* dealt with the distribution of America's wheat through Chicago, for the city at the turn of the century was the undisputed leader in the trading of grain. As in the earlier novel, Norris's concern was with what he liked to call "the Wheat itself," and it is instructive to compare two passages which come from near the ends of *The Octopus* and *The Pit* respectively:

> *But the WHEAT remained.* Untouched, unassailable, undefiled, that mighty world force, that nourisher of nations, wrapped in Nirvanic calm, indifferent to the human swarm, gigantic, restless, moved onward in its appointed grooves.[7]

> And all the while above the din upon the floor, above the tramplings and the shoutings in the Pit, there seemed to thrill and swell that appalling roar of the Wheat itself coming in, coming on like a tidal wave, bursting through, dashing barriers aside, rolling like a measureless, almighty river.[8]

These highly rhetorical outbursts come after the petty personal worlds of the novels' protagonists have disintegrated irrevocably, destroyed by cosmic forces whose magnitude the "busy monster manunkind" cannot begin to comprehend. This was the heart of the naturalist's creed: man neither the center of the universe nor of attention. Norris's contemporary, the brilliant Stephen Crane, embodied the attitude in a mordant little verse that has become the epigraph to American naturalism:

> A man said to the universe:
> "Sir, I exist!"
> "However," replied the universe,
> "The fact has not created in me
> "A sense of obligation."

The naturalistic scheme requires that the protagonists in its dramas not prevail, not, that is, be heroes—except that in battling nature and losing they are to be distinguished from their even more pitiful fellow men. Of Curtis Jadwin, the defeated speculator at book's end, it is said, "the wheat itself beat him.... no combination of man could have done it" (p. 396). But in the final analysis, when it came to Chicago and the wheat, even a man among men was bound to be treated like the proverbial leaf in the gale. And so it turned out with Curtis Jadwin.

But what has the place Chicago got to do with this rather abstract drama? Interestingly enough, there is more of the Chicago scene in *The Pit* than one might expect. Of course, the Board of Trade is represented in nearly every chapter, but Norris goes further, striving for the kind of local yet symbolic effect that had already become traditional in the work of writers like Hamlin Garland and Henry Blake Fuller. The opening chapter of *The Pit* takes place in Louis Sullivan's Auditorium Theatre—the same place where Rose of Dutcher's Coolly first heard "the voice of Wagner" and fell in love. On Norris's magical night the music is Verdi, but the conversation inevitably turns to the big news at the Board of Trade:

> "—and I guess he'll do well if he settles for thirty cents on the dollar. I tell you, dear boy, it was a *smash!*"
> "—never should have tried to swing a corner. The short interest was too small and the visible supply was too great."
> Page nudged her sister and whispered: "That's the Helmick failure they're talking about, those men.... Mr. Helmick had a corner in corn and he failed today" (p. 8).

Whispers from the Pit intrude everywhere in the Auditorium, eclipsing the glory of the music and deflecting even Laura Dearborn's attention. As with Rose, this is her first opera, and she, too, is destined to fall in love in Sullivan's grand building that night. Yet art is in full retreat in the face of Helmick's failure—another corner dramatically broken and the speculator-princes gather in the halls of culture to discuss what's really important: business. Nonetheless, the operatic moment is formative for Laura Dearborn, who knows or cares little for corners in corn or wheat futures, and as she leaves the Auditorium in a carriage bound for the North Side she is pondering both the music and the presence of Curtis Jadwin, the man she will soon love and eventually marry. What she does not yet know is that he is destined to become the Chicago speculator of speculators, that Curtis Jadwin's infatuation with the Pit will bring him low and destroy her romantic ideals of beauty and the hero.

That particular evening, however, she is given a portent of the power beyond art and humanity which centered on LaSalle Street. As her party turned off Jackson onto LaSalle, "abruptly her reflections were interrupted."

> The office buildings on both sides of the street were lighted from basement to roof. Through the windows she could get glimpses of clerks and book-keepers in shirt-sleeves bending over desks. Every

office was open, and every one of them full of a feverish activity. The sidewalks were almost as crowded as though at noontime. Messenger boys ran to and fro, and groups of men stood on the corners in earnest conversation. The whole neighborhood was alive, and this, though it was close upon one o'clock in the morning! (pp. 39–40).

Anyone who has walked through the Loop's echoing financial district streets at night, cavernous and eerily deserted, can imagine the effect of this midnight conclave on LaSalle Street, its feverish activity in a darkness broken only by the unnatural lights from the offices like some coven in the urban forest. The prospect "stupefied" Laura and forced upon her a new understanding: "Ah, this drama of the 'Provision Pits,' where the rush of millions of bushels of grain, and the clatter of millions of dollars, and the tramping and the wild shouting of thousands of men filled all the air with the noise of battle! Yes, here was the drama in deadly earnest—drama and tragedy and death, and the jar of mortal fighting. And the echoes of it invaded the very sanctuary of art" (p. 40). And the young woman's last impression was an atmospheric glimpse of the center of the maelstrom, the Board of Trade Building:

> Laura turned and looked back. On either side of the vista in converging lines stretched the blazing office buildings. But over the end of the street the lead-coloured sky was rifted a little. A long, faint bar of light stretched across the prospect, and silhouetted against this rose a sombre mass, unbroken by any lights, rearing a black and formidable facade against the blur of light behind it.... the pile of the Board of Trade Building, black, grave, monolithic, crouching on its foundations, like a monstrous sphinx with blind eyes, silent, grave,—crouching there without a sound, without a sign of life under the night and the drifting veil of rain (p. 41).

The end of Chapter One of *The Pit* is as fine an evocation of the symbolic power of place as exists in Chicago literature. Norris has deftly designed the scene to emphasize cultural ironies of the city. There is the obvious contrast between the Auditorium Theatre and the Board of Trade, an architectural and institutional contrast, between art and business, between refined and raw power. Then there is the personal consciousness of Laura Dearborn, nicely primed by her evening's experiences to take it all in. Finally, there is the chilling suggestion of evil in the contrast between the unnaturally lighted and active LaSalle Street offices and the dominating blackness of the watchful Board of Trade at the end of the avenue. If the role of the social novel is to personalize the big issues of the day in a credible and realistic dramatic context, then we may conclude that Norris got a splendid start in *The Pit.* Its opening pages establish both an exciting Chicago scene and an expectant mood for the larger-than-life story to come.

Curtis Jadwin's Faustian attempt to control the uncontrollable is a fascinating and not too farfetched core for the novel. Norris himself seems more taken with the irresistible forces of the Pit than with the love story of Laura and Jadwin. Neither creator nor protagonist can resist its attraction: "Try as he would, the echoes of the rumbling of the Pit reached Jadwin at every hour of the day and night. The maelstrom there at the foot of LaSalle Street was swirling now with a mightier rush than for years past. Thundering, its vortex smoking, it sent its whirling far out over the country, from ocean to ocean, sweeping the wheat into its currents, sucking it in, and spewing it out again in the gigantic pulses of its ebb and flow" (p. 259).

As we have seen, the suggestion of moral darkness is probably not accidental, and the suggestion becomes explicit as we see Jadwin, the "Unknown Bull," drawn ever deeper into the Pit in his attempt to corner the market in wheat. His is the recurrent western hubris of overreaching the human grasp, of seeking the transcendence which has always been denied. Jadwin comes to see himself as a "Napoleon of Wheat," but the reader sadly follows the descent of his soul into monomania—a monomania that eventually leads to a total physical and psychological breakdown. And, of course, to the destructive failure of his "corner." It could only have happened in Chicago. That was where the trading was done, and in the wide-open city there was, perhaps uniquely in all of America, sufficient latitude for a heroic businessman to flex his muscles. But Chicago was a gamble, was also the only place where failure could be so complete and so devastating. The failure of the Jadwin corner forces them out of the city, he an invalid and she thoroughly disabused of romantic notions. They set out for the West, hoping to start over in the obsessive fashion of down-but-not-quite-out Americans. Should the reader have somehow missed Frank Norris's point, he concludes *The Pit* with Laura—not Jadwin—looking out of their window of their westbound train as it pulls out of the station. Of all the myriad details of the city, what does she see? "On either side of the vista in converging lines stretched the tall office buildings, lights burning in a few of their windows.... Over the end of the street the lead-coloured sky was broken by a pale faint haze of light, and silhouetted against this rose a sombre mass, unbroken by any glimmer, rearing a black and formidable facade against the blur of the sky behind it" (p. 420). The description is literally the same as the first glimpse of the Board of Trade nearly four hundred pages before, a kind of melancholy refrain to this Chicago ballad. The power of the wheat is undiminished, still unassailable in its temple at the end of LaSalle, oblivious to the lives it has consumed. Now the shadows of Jadwin and Laura leave the Pit and the city behind, hopeful but hardly optimistic about their future. To the West. And it is the final measure of the cultural maturity of Chicago, in fiction and fact, that the great city itself has ceased to be a symbol of the West and is, instead, indisputably in the center.

Carl Sandburg and the Turning toward Poetry

It is a curious fact that the strain of the local novel with which we have been concerned, both rural and urban, seemed to peter out around the time of World War I and never regained the energy or authority it had had in the 1890s. At the same time the vanguard of a new regional poetry appeared in Chicago: Harriet Monroe in 1912 founded *Poetry: A Magazine of Verse* and in so doing provided the vehicle which was to do more to revolutionize American poetry than any other. And in 1914 a native of Galesburg, Illinois, who was trying Chicago on for size published in *Poetry* magazine an emphatic lyric that began like this: "Hog Butcher for the World, / Tool Maker, Stacker of Wheat, / Player with Railroads and the Nation's Freight Handler; / Stormy, husky, brawling, / City of the Big Shoulders."[9] The poem was, as nearly everyone by now knows, "Chicago," and it continued in free verse the dynamic stereotype of the city that had been earlier established in the rhapsodic prose of Theordore Dreiser and Frank Norris.

Sandburg, a country boy and a wanderer and a genuine adherent to the American proletariat whether agricultural or industrial, was every bit as moved by Chicago as his older contemporaries, for it played upon his romantic love of magnitude and intensity, a love perhaps born of his Scandinavian roots: Chicago was the stuff of saga and he would sing it in verse as his fellows had already done in prose. Yet Carl Sandburg, as the epigraph to this section shows, did not accept Chicago's excesses or injustices uncritically. The strong currents of sentiment he felt for the common man underwent a chemical change to irony and even occasionally bitterness when he saw an urchin on a curb or a washerwoman bent clear to the ground with travail or a factory worker pale from long being shut out of the sun's healthy light. His first collection of verse, *Chicago Poems* (1916), reveals the attraction-repulsion conflict he would always have with Chicago. Readers more accustomed to the machismo-like "Chicago"—anthologized in virtually every anthology of American poetry and often the only Sandburg poem they know—will be shocked and touched by the insistent social criticism of poems like "Mill-Doors":

> You never come back.
> I say good-by when I see you going in the doors,
> The hopeless open doors that call and wait
> And take you then for—how many cents a day?
> How many cents for the sleepy eyes and fingers?
>
> I say good-by because I know they tap your wrists,
> In the dark, in the silence, day by day,
> And all the blood of you drop by drop,
> And you are old before you are young.
> You never come back.

Here was a sensibility akin to Upton Sinclair's, and indeed Sandburg was as imbued with socialist principles as the author of *The Jungle*, though he took pains to keep overt political propaganda out of his literature. These "mill-doors" were recognizably those that had absorbed so many thousands of new Chicagoans from Europe and the native America countryside—the Jurgis Rudkuses and Sister Carries, who were the fictional representatives of the anonymous masses. Theodore Dreiser, to be sure, allowed Caroline Meeber to emerge from her factory one day and leave it behind for a long career of sexual opportunism and the theater, but she was clearly the exception: her unnumbered co-workers remained to give out their life's blood "drop by drop." It was already becoming a familiar story in American literature and life, and Carl Sandburg was the first to embody the working-person's anguish within poetry of high lyric quality.

Long after the braggadocio of the opening poem, "Chicago," has subsided, it is the people of *Chicago Poems* who stay in the mind's eye. They are neither the eccentric folk of *Spoon River* nor the grotesques of *Winesburg* but rather the downtrodden and despised of the city, tricked and manipulated by a class system that was the more onerous because, according to the democratic dogma, it was not supposed to exist. For Sandburg knew his Marx, knew as well the rhetorical tricks for elucidating the class struggle without polemics. There is Mrs. Gabrielle Giovanitti of "Onion Days," who "comes along Peoria Street every morning at nine o'clock / with kindling wood piled on top of her head, her eyes looking straight ahead to find the way for her old feet." This she does each and every weary day, while her widowed daughter-in-law picks onions for ten or maybe twelve hours a day out on Bowmanville Road, slaving for one Mr. Jasper:

> Last week she got eight cents a box, Mrs. Pietro Giovanitti, picking
>   onions for Jasper,
> But this week Jasper dropped the pay to six cents a box because so
>   many women and girls were answering the ads in the *Daily News.*
> Jasper belongs to an Episcopal church in Ravenswood and on
>   certain Sundays
> He enjoys chanting the Nicene creed with his daughters on each side
>   of him joining their voices with his.
> If the preacher repeats old sermons of a Sunday, Jasper's mind
>   wanders to his 700-acre farm and how he can make it produce
>   more efficiently.
> And sometimes he speculates on whether he could word an ad in the
>   *Daily News* so it would bring more women and girls out to his
>   farm and reduce operating costs.

The ploy is to make Mrs. Giovanitti and her daughter-in-law real and sympathetic, while Jasper is seen as the stereotyped greedy capitalist exploiter—Charles Dickens by way of Karl Marx. Sandburg lets us know that in spite of it all "Mrs. Pietro Giovanitti is far from desperate about life," for she has that same quality of mythic endurance earlier seen in Sinclair's Lithuanians, and, for that matter, in Zury Prouder down in Spring County. Agrarian peasants become urban proletarians; but wherever they are they remain tenacious. Perhaps it should be emphasized that Sandburg was attempting a radical sort of poetry. He filled it with the unanswerable righteousness of the class struggle, the result sounding more than a little like the black "poetry of rage" of the late 1960s. To the black poets the fact of American racism was as clear as that of class prejudice was to Sandburg, and if you make Jasper a slum landlord in the black urban ghetto his indictment for social irresponsibility would be the same. Moreover, "Onion Days" has one other characteristic of radical poetry: its subject is felt by the author to be "too human" for use in conventional bourgeois literature.

> I listen to fellows saying here's good stuff for a novel or it might be
>   worked up into a good play.
> I say there's no dramatist living can put old Mrs. Gabrielle
>   Giovanitti into a play with that kindling wood piled on top of her

head coming along Peoria Street nine o'clock in the morning (p. 14).

The inconsistency of having just done the impossible is apparently excused by Sandburg's own ideological purity and unbiased intimacy with the Giovanittis of Chicago. And so old Mrs. Gabrielle staggers down Peoria Street and out of our sight—the perfect American city equivalent of Millet's "Man with a Hoe," better even than Edwin Markham's more famous verses inspired directly by that painting.

Chicago Poems presents the incandescent social conscience of Carl Sandburg more boldly and effectively than most of his later poetry, and in this "first full flush" he was much like the older Hamlin Garland, whose radicalism a generation earlier had had the same quality of a ringing social manifesto for artists. Yet by no means all of the *Chicago Poems* reflect urban social concerns: the well-known "Fog," for example, shows the imagistic concern with economy and intensity that was at the other end of the poetic spectrum from "Hog Butcher for the World." And now and then there is a poem that combines a resonant image of place with a deft suggestion of social empathy. "Subway" does more to crystallize the modern urban condition than all the louder and longer poems put together. It helps make Carl Sandburg our contemporary, puts him closer to us than the sixty intervening years would indicate:

> Down between the walls of shadow
> Where the iron laws insist,
>   The hunger voices mock.
>
> The worn wayfaring men
> With the hunched and humble shoulders,
>   Throw their laughter into toil (pp. 8–9).[10]

Carl Sandburg had an influence on American poetry, especially in the Midwest, which seems to us today all out of proportion to his literary reputation, which rests not on his poems but solidly on his Lincoln biography. But to other poets, struggling in obscurity to gain a hearing for any sort of poetry beyond newspaper versification, the publication of *Chicago Poems* was a revelation. One who was transformed by the experience of reading Sandburg was a Kansas-born lawyer in Chicago who was soon to write a momentous collection of Illinois poems himself: Edgar Lee Masters, actually ten years older than Sandburg, was the definitive late bloomer. He had fooled around with conventional high-toned verse for years, even publishing a few volumes that generated some local reputation for him. Then Masters got hold of an issue of *Poetry* in which appeared several of Sandburg's early poems, including "Chicago." The year was 1914. Masters was in his mid-forties and finally ready to begin as a poet in earnest. The immediate result of his involvement with Sandburg's work was *Spoon River Anthology* (1915), graveyard songs in the free verse that Whitman had pioneered and Sandburg had lately revived. Harriet Monroe, who knew both poets well, remembered that Masters had conceived *Spoon River* after his mind, "already shaken out of certain literary prejudices by the reading in *Poetry* of much free verse, especially that of Mr. Carl Sandburg, was spurred to more active radicalism through a friendship with that iconoclastic champion of free speech, free form, free art—freedom of the soul."[11] Ironically, *Spoon River* was in the bookshops before Sandburg's own first collection, but the sense of the latter's being the mentor is nonetheless accurate.

What with the sensations of Masters's and Sandburg's free-verse poetry, with Theodore Dreiser bringing out his fictionalized biography of Charles Yerkes (*The Titan*, 1914), and with the influx of a host of socialist writers headed by Floyd Dell, Chicago was humming with literary and ideological activity. This was the genesis of the so-called Chicago Renaissance, the literary phenomenon that established the city permanently as a legitimate cultural center.[12] Chicago from 1915 onward would never need to show embarrassment at having literary folk within its ample city limits, for it really had become the city of the big shoulders, with the twentieth century having knocked from them almost all the chips of provincialism. But had the forward-looking practitioners of the renaissance taken the time to glance backward they might have seen in the hazy past the foundations of a Chicago literary tradition which meant more to their own radical departures than perhaps they suspected. Fuller and Garland and Herrick had not wrought in Chicago for nothing, and to their generation goes the credit for the spadework and the caissons on which Sandburg and the moderns built so high. Maybe for this reason we see—when we see the picture in the fullness of its time—the nineteenth-century writers as the grandfathers and the early moderns as the fathers of our contemporary culture. And through that peculiar knack we have of skipping generations we tend to regard the grandfathers as in many ways closer to our own values and beliefs. This may be an exaggeration. But what is not is that it is psychically necessary for the continuation of Illinois and midwestern culture to see the radicalism of Sandburg and his circle as a linking force between the nineteenth century and the later twentieth. No one generation, no matter how revolutionary their work may seem in its infancy, can or ought to lop off the past, thinking it a vestigial organ the social body may now do without. This is the iconoclastic pride of every radical in art; it was the tendency of the young Garland in the 1890s and the earnest desire of a white-hot Carl Sandburg a quarter of a century afterward. It would be felt again in the proletarian writing of the 1930s, in Farrell's *Studs Lonigan* trilogy and in the dozens of now-forgotten writers who insisted that Chicago and America were, in the depression, blasphemous betrayals of the people. Yet that outcry was the third and by no means the last in a series that began with Garland's *Crumbling Idols* in 1894. One wonders if any of the troubled writers of the 1930s had heard of Hamlin Garland, who was, ironically, still living in their midst, though in obscurity. If they looked back to his fresher age, then to Sandburg's and finally to their own again, they should have been consoled by the realizations that a viable regional culture, a "usable past," was at hand and that, if history could show anything with certainty, a curative critical voice would answer when the hard times called.

NOTES-CHAPTER VI

1. Upton Sinclair, *The Jungle* (New York: New American Library, Signet Classics, n.d.), p. 349. Subsequent references are contained within the body of the essay.
2. *The Jungle* was serialized before its book publication in *The Appeal to Reason*, a national organ of the socialists published in Girard, Kansas; and it was reviewed in the same paper by Sinclair's fellow novelist and socialist, Jack London, who dubbed it "The 'Uncle Tom's Cabin' of wage-slavery.... It is alive and warm. It is brutal with life. It is written of sweat and blood, and groans with tears. It depicts not what man ought to be, but what man is compelled to be in our world, in the twentieth century."
3. Walter Rideout, *The Radical Novel in America, 1900-1954* (New York: Hill and Wang, American Century Series, 1966), p. 34.
4. Students in a class I taught at Chicago City College in the late 1960s, composed of middle-class adults (mostly Afro-Americans and second-generation Americans of European descent) were obliged to reevaluate their attitudes toward race and class after learning the "history lesson" of *The Jungle*.
5. The autobiographies of European immigrants and their descendants, fictional and otherwise, constitute a fascinating subgenre of American literature. Particularly interesting are Edward Bok's *The Americanization of Edward Bok* (1920), Abraham Cahan's *The Rise of David Levinsky* (1917), and the much more recent *Making It* by Norman Podhoretz. All these leave the reader feeling that more is lost than gained in Americanization.
6. The present Board of Trade Building, looming large at the southern end of LaSalle Street, with a statue of Ceres, goddess of grain, at the top, was built in 1930 in the undistinguished monolithic concrete style of the day. The

original building (1886)—at the same location—looked for all the world like an ornate cathedral and was among the most imposing buildings in the financial district (see the photograph in Mayer and Wade, *Chicago: Growth of a Metropolis*, p. 132).

7. Frank Norris, *The Octopus* (New York: Signet New American Library, 1964), p. 458.

8. Frank Norris, *The Pit* (New York: Doubleday, Page and Co., 1903), p. 388. Subsequent references are contained within the body of the essay.

9. Carl Sandburg, *Complete Poems* (New York: Harcourt, Brace and World, 1950), p. 3. All cited poems are from this edition.

10. Readers may wish to compare "Subway" with a much more purely imagistic poem, on the same subject and written in the same year (1916): Ezra Pound's "In a Station of the Metro"—

> The apparition of these faces in the crowd;
> Petals on a wet, black bough.

11. Quoted in *The Letters of Carl Sandburg*, ed. Herbert Mitgang (New York: Harcourt, Brace and World, 1968), p. 102.

12. A lively and engaging literary history of the time is Dale Kramer's *Chicago Renaissance* (New York: Appleton-Century, 1966).

The Road Down from Spoon River

They call it regional, this relevance.
—William Stafford

Route 9 west from Bloomington, looking for something like Spoon River: a necessary pilgrimage into the country where a lasting part of the Illinois mythology was conceived. Nowadays the highway is always busy, but the secondary roads are quiet and I follow them without design until the pastoral landscape of the river valley begins to take hold. Over the years, including recent years living in central Illinois, the name "Spoon River" has meant to me the spectral realm of Edgar Lee Masters's poems, not lines on a road map or state parks or folklife festivals. My Spoon River is dark. Yet this place I have come to now is spacious and sunny, lovely in a way very different from the necropolis of the book. Soon I abandon the car for a short climb to a little township cemetery, complete with its oak-grove, at the crest of a rounded hill. There is something melancholy—expected and appropriate—in the early springtime air. The rank grass and bright pink phlox stand in startling contradistinction to the graves and their weathered stones. Am I standing at the source of Spoon River? The reasonable answer is no, it is a romantic notion to suppose that Masters got his inspiration from walking around in this or any other cemetery. Thus far reason. But, unreasonably, I continue to think, walking from grave to grave, that these sleepers may be the very ones Masters put into the ground above Spoon River, and here they remain, well pleased with this land and this landscape, immeasurably preferring its elemental quality of refuge to painful consciousness in the town below. For in the end it was the town they hated, the narrow institutions that confined, the meager civilization that starved them. Down in the town the discontents (who epitomize Spoon River for the contemporary reader, though they are not its whole story) could find nothing to affirm in their lives, and if to live is to have a voice, they lived most fully in the brief moment when death allowed them to speak to the world.

The timeless poetic convention of the epitaph proved a neat device. The late citizens of Spoon River were at last free to size up the town, without reserve and beyond the censure of the ladies' aid or the chamber of commerce. In this sense, no doubt, every cemetery has the makings of a Spoon River. At my feet is the once-high Victorian obelisk of a leading family's plot tumbled into ruin. Close by is the residuum of an early settler's stone, far too worn by now to give up its modicum of information—what was surely a pious verse above, names and dates below. "All, all, are sleeping on the hill." Actual and fictive folk commingle in an imagination that can no longer distinguish the book of Spoon River from Spoon River itself.

As Illinois goes, this place is old. A few of the graves antedate the Civil War. A few reflect its ravages. And many more recall the waving of the bloody shirt in yearly celebrations to the turn of the century and beyond. Going further back, somewhere on this hilltop acre is reputedly the final western home of a Revolutionary sergeant who wandered out of Rhode Island in 1805, eventually found himself in Illinois, and became for years a fixture in the town's Independence Day parade, marching down Main Street to the tattoo of his own different drummer, marching long after he had ceased to know exactly what he was doing and the town had other wars to fight and remember. But I search in vain for the plain old soldier in the midst of the high-rise Gilded Age monuments and Grand Army of the Republic memorials. It occurs to me, and not for the first time, that the nineteenth century is a strange, vast distance away, with no bridge of ages for convenient crossing back and forth. Here, though our generations have their occasional markers, and a number of the old stones have been replaced by new monoliths of polished granite, "history" appears to have begun with Lincoln's progenitors and to have ended sometime around 1900. We talk easily about continuity with the past and try to possess it through the simplifications of genealogy and hereditary clubs devoted to American ancestor-worship. And in so doing we get a version of the past that tells us precisely what we want to know; it looks and tastes familiar because it is from our own recipe. But what of the *other* past, the one with so many ingredients that aren't handy and some few that we shall never find? The myth of continuity, if it is to serve us in health, must be taken entire. The myth must help us make not only those self-aggrandizing connections between past and present, which beguile us into thinking that Lincoln was only yesterday and hence is with us yet, but also an approach to this perplexing otherness—a palpable difference that suggests an *ancient* Illinois, a vanished aboriginal race, with as yet no key for deciphering its traces in such high places of symbolism as graveyards.

In bewilderment I am inclined to return to the literature of the towns and locales of the Midwest for what may be a more direct route to the other culture. Masters's *Spoon River Anthology,* for better or worse our classic of classics, efficiently goes about the business in which literature excels both archaeology and history: its poems reduce the social and ethical complexity of a human community to a structured view, in this case one that is often negative to the point of misanthropy. No one who has read these bitter capusles of hatred or despair is likely to forget them:

> I loathed you, Spoon River, I tried to rise above you,
> I was ashamed of you. I despised you
> As the place of my nativity.[1]

The failed sculptor Archibald Higbie had lived in Rome, where he prayed every day for "another / Birth in the world, with all of Spoon River / Rooted out of my soul," but nothing like this ever came to the deracinated artist, who ended up back in the home ground for good. Even in Italy he had been "weighted down with western soil," and whenever he tried to sculpt Apollo he inexorably got a "trace of Lincoln." Do we sympathize with Higbie and feel the shock of recognition in his miserable life? When I was in college we were supposed to rage with Higbie against the town in the way we walked desperately on the beach with Hesse's Steppenwolf, but things have changed. Now that I know there's more to midwestern literature than Spoon River. Higbie's self-pity reminds me of another expatriate, Francis Grierson in London, for whom the ghost of Lincoln was also an unshakable heritage, though he turned the matter of Lincoln to triumphant account, the weight of western soil proving no burden but a kind of hothouse blessing when, further from his roots than Masters or Higbie, he needed to write another and a better book about nineteenth-century Illinois, *The Valley of Shadows.* Grierson's rhapsodic evocation of the 1850s is still moving and immediate, but Masters's Higbie whines from lack of talent and gumption—two qualities the despised Spoon River could not be expected to provide.

A more righteous case against the town is brought by its aspiring women. Many of them struggled toward identity only to be beaten down. There was Minerva Jones, for example, unprepossessing, ridiculed

on the streets, a sometime newspaper poetess, who was brutalized by one
"Butch" Weldy, then turned over to Doc Meyers, who bungled the
abortion and had to watch her die, "growing numb from the feet up."
Her last behest is that someone "go to the village newspaper / And
gather into a book the verses I wrote" (p. 44). This was never done.

Or Margaret Fuller Slack—the name says it all—who "would have
been as great as George Eliot / But for an untoward fate": namely, marrying the druggist John Slack, who promised her leisure for her novel but,
as soon as the wedding was over, commenced getting children on her to
the number eight. Writing was obviously out of the question, though
before long it didn't matter:

> It was all over with me, anyway,
> When I ran the needle in my hand
> While washing the baby's things,
> And died from lock-jaw, an ironical death (p. 70).[2]

On the slim evidence of her epitaph, Margaret Fuller Slack would never
have rivaled George Eliot, but then neither did Masters, despite his more
than fifty books. And the point in any case is that her scenes of provincial
life went unwritten: even in death her only voice was his ventriloquism.

Over and over this is the fate of Spoon River's blighted women. Once
in a while they flamed out, like Nancy Knapp, who danced and waved
her arms in madness as her house burned down from a fire of her own
setting; or they chose suicide, like Julia Miller, who wanted romantic
transcendence but not her unborn child or her elderly husband. But for
the most part they just endured in silence, until death offered a brief bitter
voice for their "stories."

What a strange necrology, poem after poem! Where are the well-
adjusted citizens of Spoon River, the ones who evidently lived in broad
daylight and had little to complain of? They are consigned to the back of
the book, arrayed in the part of the cemetery—well tended and redolent
of artificial flowers these days—through which I walk in long strides,
scarcely glancing down at the stones, on my way to the gloomier
precincts where reside the most memorable grotesques in this dark book
of failures. Failure is what literary history says is properly important
about "village virus" literature, but who today would want to claim descent from these people? How can the likes of Higbie and Minerva Jones
provide any real sense of spiritual kinship? The truth is that what was in
1915 a chilling indictment of small-town arrested development is, fifty
years on and more, merely a curiosity. Fortunately for poets and citizens

alike, the village virus has been on the retreat in the face of tough and sustained public health measures—liberal infusions of culture and bright civic-mindedness—and has been, like smallpox, all but eradicated. Today Minerva Jones's doggerel would be collected and published, if only by her relatives or the local historical society, and Margaret Fuller Slack would contrive to make time for her novel one way or another. We live much more comfortably, too comfortably Masters would probably say, and the writer's interest in the hometown tends to be more sympathetic than in his era—more sympathetic and sometimes even reverential. The mythic overlay of a half-century's progress has disarmed social criticism. The recently rediscovered materials of vernacular history and folklore can now be used unselfconsciously and without the stilted irony and verged sentimentality of old Spoon River.

Such relaxation is, I think, mainly to the good. An obvious benefit is that the humor missing from Spoon River is back, in the form of a midwestern idiom that was once a wellspring of American literature in the nineteenth century. We all know both the words and the music to this ballad of clichés from Dave Etter:

> It's certainly a lead-pipe cinch, pardner,
> that I'm in a dark blue funk.
> I can no longer root hog or die
> till the cows come home to this farm.
> You got to know the ropes to go against the grain,
> and scratchin' around in the soil
> ain't exactly my cup of Budweiser.
> But I can still cut the mustard
> and won't take no back seat
> to some highfalutin' fly-by-night dude
> who don't know if he's afoot or on horseback.
> I'm turnin' over a brand new leaf, you see.
> I've got other fish to fry
> when I get across that bright Mississippi water.
> And I ain't singin' you no tune
> the cow died of, neither.
> Remember, pardner, you done got the real goods,
> straight from the horse's mouth,
> which, while no manna from heaven,
> is nevertheless within an ace of the gospel.[3]

"Bright Mississippi" is in the familiar idiom of the riverman's brag, the setting still a tavern by the water, the message still the same as in Mike Fink's day. Yet this gentler soul of the 1970s is not really spoiling for a fight, nor itching to light out for the territory 150 years too late. He knows all he has to do is cross the beckoning bridge from Illinois to Iowa and he'll be beyond the bright Mississippi. And we and his creator know he's not going anyplace. That's the hint of pathos in an otherwise chuckling poem. The spirit is willing but we've run out of room for western heroism of the half-horse and half-alligator species. The bright image and the ritual phrases are all we've got left, but for Dave Etter this is mostly a laughing matter.

Today's imaginative atlas shows a new order of towns (though they may actually be as old as Spoon River) where life is good and there is a prominent sign forbidding tragedy posted at the city limits. Dave Etter's Alliance, Illinois, is built upon the mellower ironies of fellow feeling instead of alienation. When we meet his Michael Flanagan, unemployed and without prospects, he is sitting in his house doing what all our literary Illinoisans have seemed to do since Spoon River—composing his epitaph and preparing to go up on the hill:

> An open book is what I want chiseled
> on my marble gravestone,
> and these simple words,
> "He never got off the bus."
> Coming from a place so small
> that the tallest building
> was an Arco station,
> I should have been prepared
> to hear advice for the unemployed,
> such as the mailman's,
> "Perhaps you can catch on
> at the car wash across town."
> I gaze at the sheepskins
> tacked neatly to the wall
> and slump in my chair.
> I am an empty burlap bag now,
> the loose grain of my body
> falling on the bare floorboards,
> my tired, feeble thoughts turning
> to carnival lights blowing
> in the big Midwestern wind,
> my father coming out
> of the beer tent again,
> his Irish-American face
> red as a brakeman's flag.[4]

Flanagan could be the grand-nephew of any number of Spoon River deadbeats, but he is willing in 1975 to try a sad and knowing smile against the blankness of failure that drove his uncles to their grotesque and ineffectual antisocial behavior. Etter's latter-day towns have gas stations instead of liveries, and their post offices are closing one by one, but the corner groceries and taverns and courthouses survive to carry the same old load of human weariness. In Alliance, Illinois, Judge Emil Zangwill trudges home in the cold April rain to spend another night with Jack Daniel's, while over on another street Grover Ely muses over the decayed meaning of his "ancestral home":

> The ancestors who built this monumental brick home
> still stare, thin lips pursed, from their oval frames.
> We, the living Elys, are softer, poorer, sadder, but
> we try to stay on another year, bear another Ely child.[5]

"Softer, poorer, sadder"—the Elys are the heirs to a bankrupt tradition. Yet they will stay on another year, even though "Down in the yard the sundial has died of too much shade" and "All four chimneys are unsafe and haven't smoked in years." Why? Why stay on? Etter has a ready repertory of furtive non-answers, and none vaguer than Howard Drumgoolie's in "Hotel Tall Corn": "You know, I sorta, kinda like it"—a qualification and an accommodating middle ground never allowed in Spoon River.[6]

But to achieve a perspective Etter occasionally lets his people out of town for a brief retreat into nature: to a "forgotten graveyard" surely like my township cemetery and Spoon River, above the town and further away from it than the physical distance back.

> I have left my townsmen down below
> under the shadows of Town Hall:
> religious fakers, Republicans,
> the windbags at the barbershop.
>
> On this hill, the clean smell of skunk.
>
> The ape-faced trees crouch like gnarled bootblacks
> over the yellow tombstones;
> and there is a bird's nest—a torn blue wig.
>
> But I am at home among the dead,
> the deformed, the discolored.

A woodpecker joyfully carves his hole.

The sunset sweetens the mouth of a leaf.[7]

If there is such a thing as a tone which is both amused and elegiac, Etter's poems have it. They imply in an understated way the imminent passing of Alliance, Illinois, from the actual to the imaginative: not only is Grover Ely nostalgic (in a rather baffled way, to be sure) about his moldering ancestral home, but for the reader the very persona of such a man in such a situation is itself nostalgic. The towns I grew up in were ringers for Alliance, but they aren't like it today, and the town I now live in is busy transforming itself into something unrecognizable from the old small-town viewpoint. Every Illinois county has its ghost towns, and not all of them went to spirit way back in the collapse of the nineteenth century's expansive hopes. This is where Alliance, too, is headed, for the towns that persist into the next century will be larger, more central, more economically alive, and (no doubt) duller. They will be the "regional cities" so beloved of contemporary urban planners.

The sad part, of course, is that the more livable regions and their constituent towns become, the less they will be inhabited as places. In this crucial matter of place, no one has been more percipient than Wright Morris, the chief literary archaeologist of the Midwest, who observed some twenty years ago that "no matter where we go, in America today, we shall find what we just left."[8] And it is by now a commonplace that even the most tenacious aspects of regional culture—language and custom—are losing out to this creeping American uniformity. Certainly the physical towns, with their epidemics of franchises along Main Street and their naked subdivisions—like starting over on the treeless prairie but this time on the "amenable frontier"—are stupefyingly the same whether in Coffeyville, Kansas, or Clinton, Connecticut. The condition may seem worst in the Midwest because our towns are the most obvious (in the old literal sense of something standing smack in the middle of the road: you can't miss it) and the land is so open and extensive. We have nowhere to hide and protect what little is left of our cultural distinction.

The one midwestern difference everyone notices, and more often than not negatively remarks, is the landscape itself. On the long interstate haul across Illinois, Iowa, Nebraska, the cars often seem to drive themselves, the passengers staring like zombies at the nothingness of the agricultural plains. Yet to an inhabitant this very openness is *place*, and openness is, paradoxically, an aesthetic refuge for many midwestern poets who still feel (in James McGowan's memorable phrase) the "metaphysical prickle" of the prairie landscape.[9] Midwestern poetry of place treats the landscape as a standpoint. As William Stafford puts it, "Everything we own / has brought us here: from here we speak."[10] Stafford's advice is to "have a place, be what that place requires," and I would not underestimate the midwestern poet's abilty to blazon this as a motto with which to answer, in perennial words and images, the vagaries of fashion and taste and the generally bland homogeneity of American national culture.

I happen to live in a town where a painter named Harold Gregor does pictures of barns. The pictures are beautiful and cause comment in New York City. And in another part of the state a poet, Lisel Mueller, offers a striking (yet coincidental) poetic analogue which moralizes the archetype of Gregor's paintings:

> Look at this country,
> those shapeless multiple greens
> haphazard, inhumanly lost:
> but for the barns,
> the colorful mothers,
> settling them all like wayward children
> around their sturdy skirts,
>
> where would all that loneliness go?[11]

In "Highway 2, Illinois" the motherly barns subsume the loneliness of the land, and art mediates the lonely standpoint of men and women in the landscape. This relevance is all that Illinois, as a place, has ever had or ever needed.

Poets and painters are rightly suspicious of facile uses for art. But the work of softening the white summer glare and shaping the "shapeless multiple greens" of the Illinois landscape is something they surely must affirm. The Midwest as a unique cultural region is dying. Thus the retreat into place—into, as the familiar metaphor goes, an island in the corn—and the preservation of a usable past are more urgent matters than in former days. In the world of the quotidian I find it easy to ignore my own backyard, living with an inertial complacency that would no doubt have angered the "village virus" writers. Most of the time I do not live in a place and do not care. But once in a while, say early in April, "something startles me where I thought I was safest" and I feel the need to rediscover Illinois. Commencing in the springtime on a township cemetery hill, continuing in summer when "the whole wide land is a map," I prospect the country with a painter friend, whose geometry on canvas recalls the primal ordering act of the first surveyors—the act of enclosing the land against its being "haphazard, inhumanly lost." In abstraction he and I do again what the pioneers first did to Illinois, ordering and framing the land with straight thought. And if I dream of some breathtaking expanse of lost virgin prairie, dimensionless and shapeless and innocent of the deep cut of the plow, I am also happy to be able to imagine that wilder landscape in the regular rectangular one spreading before my eyes. This act of imagination is necessarily coeval with art: I see Illinois both through my own eyes and through the composing and tempering lenses of painting and literature.

Both kinds of seeing are important if we are to hold on. I believe we face an important choice about regional culture. We can leave, or leave in staying, and be judged for it, much as the colony of prairie dogs judged William Stafford, long after the original "Prairie Town" was gone:

> Pioneers, for whom history was walking through dead grass,
> and the main things that happened were miles and the time of day—
> you built that town, and I have let it pass.
> Little folded paws, judge me: I came away.[12]

The alternative is to remain and work to keep what is ours from passing. We must start with the "rude beginnings" of the American civilization in Illinois, with the first stunning sight of the sea of prairie as scrawled in a pioneer's diary, and trace the distinctive utterance to its contemporary center in our own backyard:

> "We're staying right here the rest of our lives," I said.
> "In Illinois?" she said.
> "That's where we are, isn't it?" I said.[13]

NOTES—EPILOGUE

1. Edgar Lee Masters, *Spoon River Anthology* (New York: Collier Books, 1962), p. 204.
2. Masters, *Spoon River Anthology*, p. 70. Masters's antidote for this despair among the women was the idealized portrait of his grandmother, "Lucinda Matlock," who is both strong and happy, no doubt because she knows her proper sphere: she was married for seventy years, raised a large family (twelve children, not the mere eight of Mrs. Slack!), and did social service by nursing the sick with herbs gathered in her wanderings over the Spoon River country. At ninety-six she dies ("I had lived enough, that's all") and passes judgment on the younger generation:

> Degenerate sons and daughters,
> Life is too strong for you—
> It takes life to love Life (p. 239).

3. Dave Etter, *Bright Mississippi* (La Crosse, Wis.: Juniper Press, 1975), n.p.

4. Dave Etter, *Cornfields* (Peoria, Ill.: Spoon River Peotry Press, 1980), pp.14–15.

5. Dave Etter, *Alliance, Illinois* (Ann Arbor, Mich.: Kylix Press, 1978), p. 62.

6. Etter, *Alliance, Illinois,* p. 63.

7. Dave Etter, "The Forgotten Graveyard," in *Heartland: Poets of the Midwest,* ed. Lucien Stryk (De Kalb: Northern Illinois University Press, 1967), p. 63.

8. Wright Morris, *The Territory Ahead* (New York: Atheneum, 1963), p. 22. The entire paragraph is worth quoting: "The *region*—the region in the sense that once fed the imagination—is now for sale on the shelf with the maple-sugar Kewpies; the hand-loomed ties and hand-sewn moccasins are now available, along with food and fuel, at regular intervals on our turnpikes. The only regions left are those the artists must imagine. They lie beyond the usual forms of salvage. No matter where we go, in America today, we shall find what we just left."

9. From his poem, "On Writing an Illinois Poem," which is printed in full as the epigraph to this book.

10. William Stafford, "Lake Chelan" and "In Response to a Question," from *Stories That Could Be True* (New York: Harper and Row, 1977), pp. 84 and 75.

11. Lisel Mueller, "Highway 2, Illinois," from *Voyages to the Inland Sea,* ed. John Judson (LaCrosse, Wis.: Center for Contemporary Poetry, 1971), vol. 1, p. 16.

12. William Stafford, "Prairie Town," *Stories That Could Be True,* p. 70.

13. Dave Etter, "Kermit Olmsted: Roots," *Alliance, Illinois,* p. 75.

Index

A Note on the Author

Robert C. Bray was born in Pittsburg, Kansas. He graduated from Kansas State College (now Pittsburg State University) and received his M.A. and Ph.D. (with honors) in English from the University of Chicago. He teaches English and American Studies at Illinois Wesleyan University, and is the author of several scholarly articles on midwestern literature and coauthor of *The Diary of a Common Soldier in the American Revolution.*